Ghost Hunting
with DEREK ACORAH

Ghost Hunting
with DEREK
ACORAH

STAR OF TV'S *MOST HAUNTED*

DEREK ACORAH

HarperElement
An Imprint of HarperCollins*Publishers*
77–85 Fulham Palace Road
Hammersmith, London W6 8JB

The website address is : www.thorsonselement.com

and *HarperElement* are trademarks of
HarperCollins*Publishers* Limited

Published by HarperElement 2005

1 3 5 7 9 10 8 6 4 2

A catalogue record for this book
is available from the British Library

ISBN 0 00 718348 8

Printed and bound in Great Britain by
Clays Ltd, St Ives plc

To my mother, Elizabeth, with love and thanks

Contents

Acknowledgements

I would like to thank all the people who continue to help and support me in my work as a spiritual medium. When difficult moments have arisen, these people have helped to keep me focused on the real reason for being here – my work for spirit, without which I would be nothing.

Special thanks go once more to LIVINGtv's Richard Woolfe and Clare Hollywood for their not inconsiderable support over the past year.

I would also like to thank all the people at Harper-ThorsonsElement and for allowing me to put into words my experiences as a spiritual medium.

Lastly, I would like to offer my thanks to the people who have been less than kind in their opinions of me. The knowledge of those opinions has helped spur me on in my work for the spirit world.

Introduction

My name is Derek Acorah. I am a medium with clairaudient, clairvoyant and clairsentient gifts. Over the years I have conducted many paranormal investigations and in this book I would like to share some of my experiences with you in the hope that it will assist the intrepid ghost hunters amongst you.

I first became aware of my ability to communicate with the world of spirit as a small boy. I was living with my family at my grandmother's house when one day I saw what I thought was a man standing on the first-floor landing. He spoke to me and as he reached out towards me, it felt as though he was ruffling my hair. I was very afraid and raced down the stairs to tell my gran that there was a strange man in the house. My gran and my mother hurried up the stairs, but there was nobody to be found.

'Tell me what the man looked like, Derek,' my gran said gently. I described the person I had seen. As I did so my mother and my gran exchanged glances. My gran took a large tin down from a shelf in the kitchen and took out a photograph. I was startled to see that this was a picture of the very man who had stopped me on the staircase.

'That's him!' I shouted. 'That's the man on the stairs!'
'He's the next,' said my gran quietly to my mother.

She explained to me that the man I had seen on
the stairs was in fact my grandfather, who had passed
to the spirit world before I was born. She told me that
I would see many, many people who had passed from
this life to the world beyond and that I wasn't to be
afraid. At the time I didn't understand. I didn't know
that my grandmother was a medium herself. I did
know that many people would come to the house to
sit and chat with her and would leave looking very
much happier than when they arrived, but I didn't
notice that it was in fact my grandmother who would
do all the talking!

Being a young lad, I soon forgot the incident and got
on with the single most important thing in my life –
football! I told everybody that I wanted to be a footballer when I grew up. As I went from junior to senior
school, it became apparent, much to my father's
delight, that I did indeed have some talent as a footballer. My dad would talk longingly about watching
me play for the team he and all my uncles revered –
Everton Football Club. His disappointment was huge
when at the age of 15 I signed as an apprentice pro with
Everton's arch rivals Liverpool.

I was a professional footballer for a number of years.
After leaving Liverpool FC I joined various other
clubs, including Wrexham, Glentoran and Stockport,
before eventually ending up in Adelaide, South
Australia, playing for USC Lion. By this time I had

met and married my first wife, Joan, and we had become the proud parents of our son Carl, who was born shortly before we left for Australia.

My footballing career came to an end in the early 1980s and I returned to the UK with my family. Although football had been my passion, I had not forgotten my early brushes with the spirit world, which I have written about in my first book, *The Psychic World of Derek Acorah*, and I now saw where my ultimate destiny lay – working for spirit. I had been allowed to achieve my childhood ambition, but now I had to take on the real work of helping others through the use of my mediumistic gifts, just as my grandmother had done before me.

Joan and I went our separate ways and, living on my own, I began conducting private readings for people. Before I knew it, I was in demand. I was working for spirit each and every day – and finding a fulfilment I had not experienced whilst playing football. I knew without a doubt that my grandmother had been correct. I was indeed 'the next one'!

I have recorded at length in my second book, *The Psychic Adventures of Derek Acorah*, how I came to meet my spirit guide, Sam, and to work in radio and television. After meeting the husband-and-wife team Yvette Fielding and Karl Beattie, who created LIVINGtv's unrivalled paranormal programme *Most Haunted*, I found myself ghost hunting all over the country. Although I had already conducted many paranormal investigations, it was during the *Most*

Haunted investigations that I honed my skills as a 'ghostbuster'. I would now like to tell you about some of my experiences and explain what ghost hunting is all about!

CHAPTER 1

Preparation

Preparation is essential for a successful ghost hunt, both to gain satisfactory evidence of any spirit activity and to rule out any other explanations. What will you need?

Equipment

As a spirit medium, I both see and hear spirit naturally. I am able to pick up events that have taken place in a building from the atmosphere there. I like to think of such events as 'photographs in time', but they are more commonly known as residual energies, emotions from times gone by that linger in the fabric of a place.

Although many paranormal groups turn to mediums for assistance in their investigations, investigators will also need to include items of a more worldly nature in their kitbags to give tangible proof of spirit activity.

A Torch

One obvious item is a torch. Take a supply of replacement batteries too – mischievous spirit presences like nothing better than to drain battery power and a hapless investigator who has forgotten to pack extra batteries could well end up fumbling around in the dark.

Notebooks and Pens

Notebooks and pens will enable you to record details of events as they occur. The worst thing to do is to rely on memory, as after a long night's investigation recall can be blurred, especially if there have been many exciting incidents.

It is also a good idea to make a rough sketch of the location before commencing an investigation, numbering rooms for ease of reference.

Plain sheets of white paper and pencils are also a necessity so that an item or 'trigger object' can be placed on the paper and its outline traced. Any subsequent movement of the object can then easily be detected. Wooden crosses of a suitable size seem to be popular as trigger objects, though any item which has an easily traceable outline may be used.

Cotton and Tape

It may be necessary to seal off certain rooms whilst tests are conducted. As security is not the issue here, simple black cotton and adhesive tape may be used.

A sealed room is the ideal location for a trigger object or for strategically placed cameras that will record any activity taking place.

Candles

Household candles should also be included in the kit, as the flickering of their flames may reveal a spirit presence. Checks should be made prior to starting the investigation to ensure that there are no draughts which could cast doubt over the cause of a flickering flame. Of course lit candles must never be left unattended purely from a safety point of view.

Flour

Prior to the investigation a raid on the kitchen cupboard should be made to acquire a bag of ordinary flour. When sprinkled over the floor this will reveal any footprints – or handprints, if sprinkled on a tabletop. A small soft brush should be used to distribute the flour over the desired area. Care should always be taken when investigating a property owned by another person and it may well be a good idea to spread the flour over sheets of old newspaper.

Walkie-Talkies

Walkie-talkies or two-way radios are a good way for investigators to keep in touch with one another during an investigation. If you are contemplating splitting up into groups, or even going off individually whilst investigating a location, it is always a good idea to be able to contact your fellow investigators.

A Thermometer

A thermometer is a must in order to detect fluctuations in the temperature of a room. I have seen large greenhouse-type thermometers used, but of course the serious ghost hunter will invest in a digital thermometer which gives the exact temperature on an 'easy to read' digital display.

An EMF Meter

An electro-magnetic field or EMF meter is worth acquiring. These measure fluctuations in electromagnetic energy. Parapsychologists and paranormal investigators are of the general opinion that spirits cause such fluctuations.

When investigating a property using an EMF meter, all sources of electricity, i.e. cabling, and all electrical devices must be carefully noted, as such items also generate electro-magnetic fields. Any fluctuations displayed on the EMF meter should then be checked against the location of the electrical wiring. Once all such electricity sources have been established, anything registering over 2.5 milligauss on the EMF meter indicates a possible ghostly presence. I have found, however, that EMF meters are not always capable of delivering an accurate indication of a spirit presence.

Pendulums and Dowsing Rods

Some ghost hunters favour the use of dowsing rods and pendulums. It is alleged that both devices can pick up the electro-magnetic energy field of a ghost.

Dowsing has been in use for many years. In ancient times, a 'Y'-shaped stick would be used to trace underground water sources. Today people tend to use a pair of specially prepared dowsing rods made of thick wire. Each rod is a basic 'L' shape but with a shorter foot and a longer upright. A rod is taken in each hand, with the shorter length held firmly in each fist and the longer end sticking straight out in front. Upon reaching an area of psychic activity, the rods will begin to swing wildly and cross over each other. Before attributing a dowsing rod reaction to paranormal activity, however, checks should be made to ensure there are no underground streams or other sources of water in the area.

It is said that most paranormal activity takes place in areas where many ley lines are present or at the junction of ley lines, so if investigators are aware of the location of these lines, they will have a clearer idea of where to commence their dowsing. To discover where these lines run, initially investigators would have to make enquiries of people at the locations or conduct prior research. They could of course spend many long hours walking backwards and forwards trying to determine the route of ley lines, but that could well be a complete waste of time as they could find that they had simply been following the route of an underground stream or water source.

Pendulums may also be used in psychic investigations. A pendulum is a length of cord which is attached to either a small weight constructed from wood or metal or, as is my preference, a small quartz crystal suspended from a light chain approximately seven or eight inches in length. Hold the end of the chain, allowing the pendulum to hang straight down. The pendulum must be completely still. It must then be asked to indicate 'yes' and 'no'. It will respond by either revolving in a clockwise or an anticlockwise direction; it may swing from side to side or backwards and forwards. It is up to each individual to establish the relevant response and its meaning, as these can differ from person to person.

Once you have established the relevant pendulum reactions for 'yes' and 'no', you can ask the pendulum many questions. It can also be used to locate psychically active areas in much the same way as dowsing rods. It will swing or spin more and more rapidly as it comes closer to psychic energy or a spirit presence.

Not all investigators use dowsing rods or pendulums, but they can add an interesting element to paranormal investigations.

A Tape Recorder

A tape recorder is a definite must, both to record events during séances and to place at strategic points within the location in order to record possible spirit activity. Over the years there have been some very interesting cases of 'electronic voice phenomenon', where people have claimed that they have caught spirit voices on tape.

Cameras

Cameras are another essential, though the choice of camera is of course a personal preference. There is an argument that people will only capture 'orbs' (the first manifestation of spirit presence), or 'life lights' as I prefer to call them, using a digital camera. I, however, have found this not to be the case. When my wife has accompanied me on investigations and has taken photographs using both digital and ordinary flash cameras, orbs have been captured with both camera types, together with many other examples of spirit activity.

At least one video camera together with a tripod really is a necessity. This may be placed in a locked-off position in a room in an effort to capture evidence of spirit presence. This may take the form of floating orbs, ectoplasm or, in rare cases, movement of furniture or other items. If two or three video cameras can be positioned in the same room, clearly surveying the whole area, so much the better. Should any movement take place, the fact that it is filmed from all angles can prove that there was no human interference. It is unfortunate that on certain occasions the movement of an object has been captured on film but because only one camera has been used there has always been the argument that 'somebody moved it' – that 'somebody' being a solid and earthly person.

Man's Best Friend

It has long been stated that man's best friend is his dog. A ghost hunter's best friend can be a dog too!

All animals are psychic. It is not by chance that a pet cat or dog will know exactly when its owner is due to walk through the front door. I have received numerous communications from people telling me that their beloved cat or dog 'always knows' when they are about to arrive home, even though they have not been following a regular pattern of behaviour. Gwen has often told me that she knows that I will be arriving home shortly because the dogs will walk over to the kitchen door and sit there waiting. I too have noticed that should Gwen be away from the home, I can put the kettle on when one of our cats stations himself on the window ledge to peer at the front gate.

Stories abound of animals who have alerted their owners to unseen presences in their homes. There have also been numerous tales of guard dogs refusing to enter certain parts of properties. One such story involves a security guard and his dog who used to regularly patrol St. John's Centre in Liverpool. The dog was a large black German Shepherd named Sabre, who was known for his fearlessness when dealing with intruders. However, there was one part of the shopping mall that Sabre refused to visit. He would strain at his lead, bark and growl when encouraged to walk there. It was a spot where an unfortunate accident had taken place during the construction of the centre. A young builder had fallen to his death and his spirit was known to revisit the scene.

It makes perfect sense to me therefore that a dog would be an excellent companion when undertaking the investigation of an allegedly haunted location. Not every dog is afraid, of course. Some dogs may acknowledge a spirit presence by wagging their tail whilst looking towards something that they can see but that you cannot. Others may bark and run up to an area where nothing is discernible to you. Others may display fear, just like Sabre, by refusing to go into or past a certain area. But if you have a dog, take it along! It can only add to the fun and provide a warm furry body to snuggle up to during those long dark vigils.

These are my suggestions for equipment to use when conducting a ghost hunt. Of course if you are technically adept, you will be able to devise your own methods. These may include buzzers, bells and alarms which will sound if activity is detected, and infra-red rays (similar to the type used in security systems) which will sound an alarm when broken. There are many ingenious devices – the choice is yours. However, with the few simple items I have mentioned, a ghost hunt may be conducted quite satisfactorily.

Other Preparations

Once you have your kitbag together, there are a few other preparations to make before starting your investigation.

It is always necessary to rule out in advance the more worldly explanations for noises or movements which could in the excitement of the moment be attributed to a ghostly presence. I recall visiting one location where the chandelier was said to swing when 'the spirits' were around. An examination of the alcove in which the chandelier hung showed loose-fitting window panes which allowed quite a strong draught through. Needless to say, 'the spirits' only made their presence felt on breezy days!

Breezes are not the only thing to look out for. Loose floorboards are an extremely common source of 'ghostly' creaks and groans. Water pipes can create some unearthly noises in the wee small hours, especially in older properties. The noise created by a badly fitting door in a draughty old house can have the hairs on your neck standing on end. Even the scurrying of mice in an old house can be mistaken for something less worldly. The branch of a tree persistently tapping on a window or roof can cause the unprepared investigator to assume that they are not alone. The natural cooling down and settlement of a house at night can create a series of noises which sound very much like footsteps ascending and descending a staircase. If a fireplace has been used, the brickwork cooling can make slight creaking and cracking noises. All these eventualities have to be taken into consideration before an investigation can commence.

If you intend using a trigger object – a cross, coin, book, etc. – it should be placed on a sheet of white paper and a pencil outline drawn around its base before the investigation begins. It is preferable to train a video camera or cameras on the object to capture on film any movement that may occur. Make sure that the whole of the sheet of paper is clearly visible so that should any movement take place, it can be proved that nobody has interfered with the item. The room should then be sealed to prevent anybody entering and inadvertently (or purposely – it has been known!) moving the trigger object.

Also in advance of the investigation taking place, a thermometer should be used to determine the naturally occurring cold and warm areas of the location. Older houses commonly had 'cold rooms' where perishable foods would be stored. Also, it may be that a certain room is warmer than the rest of the house because of the hours that the sun shines there. All things have to be taken into consideration.

Lastly, make sure that you have a map of the location so that everybody involved has a clear understanding of how the rooms relate to one another. This will ensure that when people split off into groups to investigate different parts of the location, nobody will be confused as to where they are.

CHAPTER 2

Ghostly Varieties

When researching their chosen location, the paranormal investigator can expect to find reports of different types of 'sighting'. Noises may be heard; people may see ghosts only at certain times of the year or on certain dates; people may record seeing 'just a pair of legs' or a 'headless woman'. I will describe the more common forms of paranormal event likely to be found on a ghost-hunting expedition.

Residual Energy

The more emotional or tragic the events which have taken place in a property, the stronger the energies that are absorbed by the fabric of the building. This is not to say that the normal daily life of the past is not detectable by a sensitive, but merely to explain that the more intense the emotional situation, the greater the depth of the energy. For instance, in buildings where vicious acts of murder have taken place, I have been immediately hit by the horror of the situation and at times have been forced to retreat to gather my spiritual protection around me. I have also entered buildings where nothing of any particular importance has taken place. Nevertheless, I have still been able to psychically detect the daily lives of the former occupants. I have been into old cotton mills where I was able to hear the tremendous noise of the looms and have been clairvoyantly shown the women and children at their work.

Residual energy also applies to objects. A sensitive can touch an item – maybe a piece of jewellery, a book or a piece of furniture, in fact anything which has been in contact with a person of this world or the next – and give information relating to the current or previous owner.

Anniversary Ghosts

These are the apparitions that appear at a given time on a given date each year.

The Tower of London has two famous anniversary ghosts – the phantom of Lady Jane Grey is said to reappear as a white shape every 12 February, the anniversary of her execution, and the harrowing slaughter of Margaret, Countess of Salisbury, is said to be re-enacted every 27 May.

On 19 May a coach drawn by headless horses is said to drive towards Blickling Hall in Norfolk. The figure of Anne Boleyn, cradling her bloodied head on her lap, can be seen inside. She was beheaded at the Tower of London on 19 May and was reputedly born in a house where the present Blickling Hall stands.

Another of Henry VIII's wives also appears as an anniversary ghost. On the 4 November 1541 Catherine Howard ran sobbing along what is now known as the Haunted Gallery at Hampton Court Palace, intent on pleading with the king to spare her life. Each year on this date it is said that her distraught phantom can be seen re-enacting this tragic scene.

Ghostly monks are said to walk at Glastonbury on Christmas Eve each year, while even though part of what is known as the Nun's Walk at Borley Rectory in Essex has been built upon, there are still occasional sightings of a nun on 28 July each year.

Hallowe'en (31 October) inevitably has a long tradition of anniversary ghosts, which range from First World War soldiers drinking at Bournemouth town hall to the ghostly monks who walk near the ruins of a chapel near Hitchin in Hertfordshire.

In fact there are literally hundreds of ghosts which are alleged to reappear each year on the same date. As yet I have not visited the location of an anniversary ghost on the anniversary. I have, however, been to such sites at other times and have immediately been made aware of the residual energy of some of the spirit people reputed to 'walk' the premises. One has to remember, though, that many stories of anniversary ghosts are just that – stories. They have no real truth behind them and their roots have been lost in the mists of time.

Crisis Ghosts

The theory behind crisis ghosts is that at the emotion-ally charged moment of death the spirit projects itself into the consciousness of those nearest to it in life. There have been numerous accounts of people having 'visions' of loved ones who have either been dying or been going through moments of intense fear or danger.

A well-known crisis ghost was that of Norman Leslie, a member of the famous Leslie family. During the First World War he appeared on the banks of the lake at his home, Castle Leslie in County Monaghan, Ireland. Staff at the castle thought that he had arrived home on leave and rushed to prepare his room for him, but then he was nowhere to be found. A week later his mother received a telegram informing her that he had been killed in action in France.

Ghosts who Walk through Walls

This type of ghost is usually experienced in older prop-erties, often dating back centuries, which have been altered structurally over the years. Floors may have been raised, resulting in an apparition which appears only from the knees upwards, or maybe a doorway will have been blocked up and relocated, which means that the ghost, continuing to use the original doorway, appears to walk through the wall.

I can recall investigating an old manor house in Cheshire that had been drastically altered. I was amazed to view clairvoyantly horse-drawn wagons parading backwards and forwards through the living quarters of the old house. Even more bizarre was the fact that I could only see the horses from the belly upwards, the legs being invisible.

When I related my findings to the historian present, he was able to tell me that the house had been radically altered and extended. What I was viewing was the route that carters used to take along a road which ran under the footings of the present building, hence only the upper portion of the horses and carts being visible.

Spirit People

As well as all these types of ghosts, of course there is the group of 'people' I feel particularly at home with – the spirits of people who have lived in or had a strong connection with a building and who make return visits. These are the people I can communicate with either directly or through my spirit guide Sam, who acts as an intermediary, passing on information from the people in spirit to me and enabling me in turn to pass it on to people still living in this world.

These spirit people are as alive as you and I. My truth is that there is no death – we live on in the world of spirit once we have shed the physical garb of this earthly incarnation.

Spirit people can be anywhere they wish to be. They can visit a home they used to inhabit or they can visit the homes of family members and friends. They can call in to a previous workplace to visit former colleagues or just to see how 'the old place' is being run in the present day. They turn up at theatres where mediums are demonstrating in order to communicate with loved ones in the audience. There are no restrictions on the people in the spirit world – they can go wherever they please.

CHAPTER 3

Not So Haunted

In my experience, the places that are least likely to yield a ghostly presence or the glimpse of a spirit person are the very places designed to scare the living daylights out of people by dramatizing some of the more horrific incidents of the past. I have visited a number of such places, but I am afraid to say that I have been disappointed to find that instead of experiencing a steady stream of willing spectres, I have moved between the various displays without meeting even one spirit entity.

With the growth in popularity of LIVINGtv's *Most Haunted* and paranormal programming in general, however, my mailbag has increased in size considerably and the majority of the letters I receive are genuine requests for explanations of inexplicable events taking place in people's homes. There are some communications, though, that recount events that are nothing to do with the spirit world and more to do with very fertile imaginations.

I recall with some amusement a letter I received some years ago. It was from the matron of a nursing home in Liverpool and catalogued the complaints she had been receiving from one of her elderly ladies, whom I shall name Beryl. Beryl had been complaining that she was being disturbed at night by something that she could not see. When she switched on the light there was nobody there. I decided that this was one occasion when I would go along to attempt to sort out the problem myself.

I arrived at the home and was met by the matron, who told me that she was most concerned, as Beryl was complaining loud and long to the staff within earshot of other residents, which was making everybody rather unsettled and apprehensive, especially at night.

I asked to be taken to meet Beryl and was led to the pleasant bed-sitting room that was Beryl's home.

Beryl greeted me brightly. 'Hello, Derek! I've been watching you on the telly. My grandson videos *Most Haunted* for me and I watch it in my room. I'd watch it in the main lounge, but the others won't have it on because they say it gives them the willies!'

As Beryl spoke I looked around the room. It was bright, comfortable and clean. I could feel nothing in the atmosphere to suggest that anything untoward from a paranormal point of view was taking place.

Beryl continued, 'I came to live here after my Bert passed away. I would have liked to have gone to the same place as my sister Jessie, but at the time there was no room for me there. She's been in touch just recently, though, and she tells me that there's a nice little room empty just opposite hers.'

I looked hard at Beryl. She grinned back at me and winked.

'So, tell me about what's been going on in your room,' I said.

Beryl proceeded to tell me a lurid tale about ghosts who roamed her room at night and entities who jumped onto her bed and pulled the bedclothes from her.

'I'm really frightened!' she said, winking at me again. 'You never know, the next thing is they might start interfering with me!'

I knew immediately that this was a ruse dreamed up by Beryl in an attempt to get herself moved to the same residential home as her sister. But as she had been speaking I had seen the spirit form of a man material-ize next to her armchair. He was a small round man who wore his shirtsleeves rolled up. He had an open friendly face and had been smiling as Beryl had unfolded her tale of ghosts and ghouls and things that went bump in the night.

'She's a wily old bird, my Beryl,' he said as she finished speaking. 'She'll stop at nothing to get in the same place as that sister of hers. They're very close.'

I thanked Beryl for allowing me into her room and asked the matron whether I could speak with her in the office.

'What d'you think, Derek?' she asked as we sat sharing a pot of tea and a plate of biscuits.

'I don't think that there's anything going on in Beryl's room at all,' I told her. 'In my opinion Beryl desperately wants to join her sister and she's come up with this story in an attempt to secure a move for herself.'

The matron looked surprised. 'Really!' she said. 'Well, if she's prepared to come up with a story such as this she must really be determined. I'll see what I can do. I believe her sister's resident at another of our houses. There may be a chance that I can arrange a transfer. It's not something we usually do, but I'll make a special concession on this occasion.'

Some weeks later I received a letter from Beryl asking me whether I would call to see her in her new home. I arranged to visit a few days later.

'You're very naughty!' I chided her.

Beryl giggled like a young girl. 'It was you who gave me the idea,' she said. 'All the ghosts and things going on in those spooky houses you visit on the telly – I thought it'd be worth a try! It gave all those other old fogies something to think about, anyway.' She grinned impishly. 'Seriously, though, Derek, I can't say that I'm sorry I pulled a fast one because I'm here with Jessie now, but I do truly believe that we go somewhere when we pass away. I know my Bert's waiting for me and that we'll be together again soon.'

I patted her hand. 'Of course he is, Beryl,' I told her. 'I saw him in your room at the other place. It looks as though he has the same sense of humour as you, so goodness knows what'll happen when you get together again!

CHAPTER 4

The Matter of a Ouija Board

Not all such claims are bogus, of course. I have visited many people who have been bothered by spirit visitation and have been able to help them understand what has been going on in their homes.

One such plea for help came from Eva, an elderly lady who lived alone in a flat on the outskirts of Wigan. 'I need your help,' she wrote. 'I don't know what to do. You're my only hope of finding peace.'

A week later I was standing outside the building which housed Eva's ground-floor flat. As she opened the front door I was hit by the cold and unwelcoming atmosphere.

'It's horrible isn't it, Derek?' Eva commented. 'It wasn't always like this, though. My home always used to have a lovely feel about it. Now I'd love to move, but I just can't afford to. You don't get much on a pension these days.' She smiled ruefully.

As Eva made a cup of tea for us, I looked around. The home seemed perfectly normal. There was a comfortable suite in front of the gas fire, a china cabinet against one wall and a small dining table and chairs against another wall. Everything was neat and tidy. In fact it was the typical home of an elderly lady.

There was nothing that I could see that would generate anything untoward and Eva herself was a lovely old soul. I imagined that normally she would have been bright and cheerful, but at the moment she was looking much less than happy.

Eva returned to the room carrying a tray of tea. She sat opposite me and proceeded to tell me what had been happening in her home.

'It all began about eight months ago,' she said. Since then she had been experiencing a number of things in her home which were disturbing and frightening. She was unable to sleep at night because of the loud bangs and crashing noises that she could hear coming from her sitting room as she was lying in bed. If she got up to investigate, there was nothing there. She would wake up in the morning to find her furniture moved around. The worst thing happened just as she was arriving home from a shopping trip one day. She heard a noise in her sitting room as she was hanging up her coat in the hallway and when she went to investigate she found that water was streaming down the wall of the room. She was now at the stage where she felt as though she just wanted to run away.

'I've had the council in,' she told me, 'and even the local priest came along. He was very kind, but no matter what he did, it didn't make any difference.'

I had a very strong feeling that Eva's problems were all linked to the flat above her. I asked her who lived upstairs. She told me that the flat was empty and had been so for more or less the same amount of time that she had been experiencing her problems.

'The young couple who lived in that flat were a bit odd-looking,' she said. 'I was glad to see them go really, because I didn't feel comfortable around them and they used to have some very strange-looking visitors.'

I sat back in my chair and closed my eyes. As I sat quietly I could feel Sam drawing closer to me. I heard his voice. 'Fools!' he said. 'They were fools – dabbling with ouija boards and the like!'

Ouija (which is a combination of the word 'yes' in French and German) boards have been popular since Victorian times, when invoking the spirits was considered something of a parlour game. The letters of the alphabet, the words 'yes' and 'no' and the numbers one to ten are arranged in a circle and a glass tumbler is used to point to them. Today it is possible to purchase a pre-printed board game which uses a plastic planchette as a pointer.

People sit around the table, each with a finger resting lightly on the base of the upturned tumbler. The spokesperson for the group will then request that any spirit who wishes to make contact with the group do so. This is where the immortal words 'Is there anbody there?' stem from. The theory is that should a spirit presence be summoned, that spirit person will use the energy of the people in attendance to move the tumbler around the tabletop, indicating letters of the alphabet which will spell out a name or a response to any question asked of it. It will answer 'yes' or 'no' by gliding over to those words and will give dates by visiting the relevant numbers.

I have come across incidences of people using a ouija board on numerous occasions. It may be a serious attempt to invoke a spirit, it may be idle curiosity or it may merely be a party game. Whatever the reason, it is a grave error of judgement to use one of these boards unless you are fully aware of the possible consequences. I do not like them and would not encourage anybody to use one myself.

The trouble generated by ouija begins with the fact that the people using the board are rarely conversant with the workings of spirit. They know nothing of the lower realms of the world beyond, the realms inhabited by spirits who can cause a variety of problems: all sorts of attacks, disruption in the home, items being moved, obnoxious smells, inexplicable noises – in fact just the type of annoyances that poor Eva was experiencing.

The only way to bring Eva some relief from the problem was to close the vortex or portal that had been opened by the irresponsible people who had up to recently lived in the flat above her. A vortex or portal is a 'doorway' in our ether used by spirits to enter or leave our earthly atmosphere.

I explained to Eva that the events she had been experiencing were nothing whatsoever to do with her – she had simply been the victim of other people's foolhardiness. I asked whether she would agree to me conducting a candle rite in her home. This would close the portal left in the atmosphere and would protect her and her home from further intrusion. 'Anything, Derek! I'll do anything to put an end to all this!' she replied.

I had suspected before I had left home that there might be the need for protection of this dear old soul, so I had come prepared with my candles and a plain white sheet. Eva supplied me with bowls of salt and water. I said my prayer of invocation and proceeded with the candle rite.

After this I am happy to say that Eva kept in touch with me from time to time and was able to report that she was living happily and peacefully in her home once more.

CHAPTER 5

Poltergeists

Poltergeist is German for 'noisy ghost' and poltergeistal activity is commonly linked to children, especially girls, approaching puberty who have displayed signs of psychic ability. It is generally agreed, and is also my opinion, that a poltergeist is not the manifestation of a spirit person, rather an abundance of energy generated by and drawn to adolescents or people suffering severe emotional stress.

Usually poltergeistal activity is limited to noises — rustlings, tappings, knocks and dragging sounds – but occasionally disarray can be caused within a home with items being thrown, furniture moved and obnoxious smells created. There have also been some reports of poltergeistal energy causing the person affected to levitate from their bed.

In most cases the problems subside if the affected individual is removed from the premises and reappear when that person returns. Obviously the person who is attracting the poltergeistal activity is unaware that the entity is drawing on their emotional energy.

It is unusual for poltergeistal activity to be of any duration. In some cases it lasts only for a few days; in others, a number of months.

There are always exceptions to the rule, however. This was amply demonstrated by an early 1950s case when the poltergeistal activity focused on not one person, but two, and in both cases males. The events took place at 1 Byron Street in Runcorn, Cheshire. Sam Jones and his grandson, John Glynn, then 16 years of age, shared a bedroom in the family home. One night, having just retired to bed, they heard a scratching noise coming from the dressing-table drawer. An investigation showed nothing and, thinking it might have been a mouse scared away by them opening the drawer, they both returned to their beds and thought nothing more about it. The following night, however, not only were there scratching noises but the drawers began to rattle and the dressing table moved, despite being extremely heavy.

After that numerous acts of poltergeistal vandalism took place – a clock was smashed, chairs were thrown against the wall and books flew through the air as though thrown by some invisible hand. There were many independent witnesses, including reporters from the *Runcorn Guardian* newspaper, two policemen, two Methodist ministers and various psychic researchers. No logical explanation could be given and it was declared to be a definite case of poltergeistal activity.

Over the years I have come into contact with poltergeistal activity on numerous occasions. Sometimes it has been of extremely short duration – a sudden burst of disruption that is over as soon as it has started. There have been other occasions, however, when people have become so frightened that they have moved out of their home, only to find that the disruption follows them to their new house.

One incident that I remember well involved a lady named Jean. She called me at my office sounding very agitated. She had been living together with her son Stephen, aged 12, and her daughter Lindsay, aged 15, since the breakdown of her marriage a year or so earlier. It had been an acrimonious divorce which Jean and her children had found extremely upsetting. As time had passed, however, they had come to terms with their new life and everything had seemed to be more settled. That was, until a few weeks before Jean's call to me.

Jean told me that strange things had started to happen – not very much at first, just little things like odd noises and belongings being moved. In fact initially it was more irritating than frightening. As the days turned into weeks, however, the noises had become more sinister. They seemed to be concentrated around Stephen's bedroom, which was situated above the family lounge. When Jean and her children were watching television in the lounge, it sounded as though something heavy was being dragged along the floor of the room above. On investigating, they would find that bedclothes had been disturbed and books had been thrown around the floor. Stephen became afraid to go to his bedroom to sleep. He reported that when he did so, he felt as though his bed was vibrating. On one occasion Jean told me that he had been literally thrown out of the bed. After that he had insisted on sleeping on the sofa downstairs.

Upon arrival at Jean's home, I stood outside looking at the house. It was unremarkable, but I knew psychically that all was not well within the four walls. I knocked on the door, which was opened a few moments later by Jean, looking pale and nervous. She told me that the previous night had been very bad, with a constant array of noises, squeaks and bangs that had prevented her and her children from getting any sleep at all.

'I'm at the end of my tether, Derek,' she said. 'I thought that we would be able to pick up our lives after my divorce and live happily here.'

She led me through to the lounge. I asked her to tell me exactly what had been going on and how her son and her daughter had coped after the divorce.

Jean told me that although Lindsay had been very upset, she had been able to continue with her life in a more or less regular way, maintaining her interests with her friends, and with the help and support of her teachers, her schooling had not been affected too badly. Stephen, however, had been a different matter. He had been extremely upset and had told his mother that he felt to blame for his father leaving the family to set up home with another woman. The fact that she had a son and daughter approximately the same ages as Stephen and his sister had exacerbated the problem. Stephen felt that his father had looked for another boy to be his son because he was not worthy of the position. Unfortunately, Jean was preventing her husband from visiting Stephen and Lindsay because of the deep hurt she had suffered. All in all, Stephen was a very miserable and confused boy. Jean had tried time and time again to explain to him that he had nothing to do with the family break-up, but he remained unconvinced.

Then the strange events began to take place. The first occasion was when Jean was sitting in the lounge. From the bedroom above came loud knocking noises. Thinking that Stephen was in his room, Jean went into the hallway and shouted up the stairs for him to be quiet. As she did so, Stephen answered from the kitchen, wondering what his mother was talking about. They both knew that Lindsay was out of the house visiting a friend. They rather nervously climbed the stairs and went into Stephen's bedroom. There was nothing there, though a pile of schoolbooks which had been lying on the desk was strewn over the floor. Jean assumed that the books had fallen to the floor, picked them up and put them away in the desk cupboard. They both went downstairs and thought no more about the matter.

A couple of nights later a similar incident took place – the knocking noise, the investigation of the bedroom and the books all over the floor. This time, though, Jean knew that there was something amiss. She herself had put Stephen's schoolbooks away not half an hour earlier. She also knew that both Stephen and Lindsay had been downstairs with her watching a favourite television programme when the noises had begun.

Every day something would happen. There would be banging and knocking noises and items would fall to the floor inexplicably, no matter how securely they were placed. Jean also started to notice an awful smell on the landing outside Stephen's room. Because his bedroom was next to the bathroom she thought there might be a problem with the drains, though the odour was not actually present in the bathroom itself. A visit from a plumber brought no relief, however, as he told her the plumbing system was in perfect working order.

Jean and her children became more and more frightened. It got to the point where they all shared one bedroom, as they were too afraid to sleep in separate bedrooms. A priest was called in to perform an exorcism, but if anything things appeared to intensify. When the family went to their bedroom at night they now felt that there was a sinister presence in there with them. At her wits' end, Jean contacted me.

It was clear to me that this was not the work of any spirit presence. It was poltergeistal activity – energy attracted by Stephen's deeply emotional state. It had built up over a period of time, feeding on the emotions Stephen was releasing into the atmosphere, recharging and growing each day until it had built up enough to create noises and move objects around the home.

I called upon Sam. 'The atmosphere must be cleansed,' he told me. 'The negativity must be broken down in order to diffuse the build-up of power.'

I talked to Jean and explained the situation to her. I told her that Stephen's unhappiness and insecurity were attracting the negativity into the home in much the same way that a moth was attracted to the light.

I asked her whether she could find it within herself to contact her husband and allow him to see the two children. Stephen would then be able to rebuild his relationship with his father and maybe the deep rejection he was experiencing would be dispelled. This in turn would stop him from sending out his unhappy thoughts into the ether, thus starving the energy build-up. Reluctantly, Jean agreed. In the meantime, I conducted a candle rite in order to cleanse the house of negativity. That, together with Stephen's happier thoughts in the weeks to come, would diminish the negativity to a point where it would disappear completely.

I visited the home on three consecutive days. Each time I performed a candle rite and prayed for the family to be relieved of the burden they were enduring. Meanwhile Jean contacted her former husband and agreed that he could once again play a part in their children's lives. Stephen became much happier once he found that his father still loved him just as much as he ever did.

Starved of the unhappy emotions Stephen was releasing into the atmosphere, the energy lost its power, and as suddenly as the unpleasantness had begun, it stopped. The family were at peace once more. The situation may not have been exactly as Stephen would have wished, but at least he knew that he could see his father and that he still loved him.

CHAPTER 6

Ghostly Communication

I am fortunate. I am both clairvoyant and clairaudient, which means that I can both see and hear spirit people. If a person who has passed into the world beyond wishes to speak to me, they can do so. However, I cannot command or demand that they do so. I cannot order a spirit person to suddenly appear and speak to me. I can only ask, and if they wish to do so, then they will. I communicate with them either directly or through Sam. If it happens that a spirit person has not been over on the other side long enough to learn how to communicate with me directly, they will tell Sam what they want to say and he will pass on their messages to me. As I have said, I am fortunate.

If a person in this world does not have the gifts I and other mediums possess, then the people in spirit have to show their resourcefulness by communicating using other methods. A common method of bringing themselves to the attention of those in this world is through the sense of smell. How many times have you been in a room and thought that you smelled the aroma of pipe smoke or the scent of a flower? How many times have you fancied that you have smelled the perfume of a loved one who has passed on to the spirit world? This is your family members communicating. They use familiar smells to bring themselves to your mind – maybe the smell of a pipe smoked by a grandfather, of the cigarette brand used by a favourite uncle, of a newly baked pie brought by a grandmother whose house always smelled of cooking. They all evoke our memories and bring to mind the loved one who is trying to let us know that they are around us always.

Another method commonly used by people in the spirit world to draw our attention to them is the movement of objects. So an ornament that was once the property of a loved one may have inexplicably moved, a curtain may twitch in a draughtless room or a framed photograph may fall over. These are all ways in which our loved ones in spirit let us know that they are still around, caring for us and guiding us.

There are also times when a spirit person who is unknown to us may wish to let us know that they are around. This is often experienced in hotel rooms, especially when the hotel was once a home. A kettle may suddenly switch itself on or a wardrobe door may swing open for no apparent reason. It is merely a former resident letting you know that they are still visiting their home or a special place which holds a particular memory for them.

Séances

The word *séance* (French for 'a sitting') is used to describe a group of people gathered together for the sole purpose of invoking a spirit or spirits from the world beyond ours. I consider it important that such a group is headed by an experienced medium, though this is not absolutely necessary.

The people involved, usually six to eight in number, arrange themselves in a circle. I find that better results are achieved if the same people take part each time. A table may be used. This is not a necessity, though it is preferable.

The people taking part must place both feet on the floor – there must be no crossed legs or ankles. This is to ensure a clear channel for spirit communication. The physical body is surrounded by an energy field known as the aura, or auric field. In order to help a spirit person to communicate during a séance it is important that there are no restrictions on that energy field. If a person crosses their legs or ankles whilst taking part in a séance this would result in what I would call a 'crossed energy polarity'. Any person taking part in a séance needs to be in tune and in balance to receive the best spirit communication.

The people involved should either join hands or, if a table is being used, should place their hands palms down upon its surface with the little finger of each hand touching the little finger of their neighbour on either side, thus maintaining a chain of energy. Everyone should be relaxed and comfortable.

The people should then close their eyes and empty their minds of all thoughts, whilst the medium, as head of the circle, recites a prayer of invocation and protection for both themselves and the people taking part in the séance. It is imperative that this is done. When invoking the spirit realms it is impossible to predict the nature of the spirit or spirits who will come.

Once contact with the spirit world has been established through the medium it is no longer absolutely necessary to maintain physical contact with the neighbouring person and people may rest their hands on their lap or on the tabletop, but with the palms upwards. This is also so that there are no restrictions on the auric field. Sitting with the palms of the hands facing upwards keeps the energy field of the physical body open. If a person were to sit with their hands clasped together or arms crossed, then that is again a crossed energy polarity.

The first sign of spirit presence is usually a noticeable drop in the temperature in the room, or even a cold draught which can be felt passing around the circle of people. The medium will then attempt to communicate with the spirit entity.

A séance should end with the head of the group thanking the spirit communicator(s) for their presence and efforts. It is at this time that any spirit entity should go back to the spirit realms that they inhabit. To help them achieve this, a prayer of thanks and protection should be offered. This could be the Lord's Prayer or any other prayer which is considered appropriate.

A séance should not be confused with the 'circles' held in Spiritualist churches or meetings. These are held for the development of mediumship. There are also 'rescue circles', which are when established mediums try to bring peace to earthbound entities and enable them to pass into the light of the higher side of life, and 'healing circles', when members of the Spiritualist church community gather together to request healing for people who are sick or needing the help of the world of spirit in overcoming the difficulties that are sometimes brought onto our life's pathway.

Many years ago I used to sit regularly in circles, one of which was a development circle for up-and-coming mediums. There were seven of us, four ladies and three gentlemen. We sat once a week on a Thursday evening in a room at my home. After a couple of weeks together as a group we started having very good results with our spirit communications.

One particular evening one of our sitters did not arrive and we decided to go ahead without her. We were ten minutes into our communication before one of the group, John, sank into a deep trance, allowing his spirit guide communicator to transfigure him. It was a sheer joy to experience – that is, until his guide informed us that Susan, the lady who had not arrived that night, had been travelling to my home when her car had skidded off the road, ending up in a ditch in the countryside.

I asked John's spirit guide whether he could give us any more information. He said that Susan had been badly injured and had been taken to hospital. Alice, her grandmother in spirit, had watched over her in the ambulance. He also told us the name of the hospital.

I asked one of the sitters to leave the circle to get in touch with the hospital. They confirmed that Susan was there and said that she had been taken straight through to the operating theatre. We decided to check that her family had been informed. I thanked the spirit guide for talking to us. He told us that on the way to the hospital Susan's heart had ceased beating on two occasions. The ambulance crew had done a good job and resuscitated her successfully. He then informed us that it was not Susan's time to leave this physical life, that she had a lot of years left. I thanked him again and closed the circle for the evening.

In the coming days we all went to the hospital to sit with Susan, who was still unconscious, and her family. We tried to reassure them that she would pull through and return to full health, although I appreciate that at the time this may have been difficult to believe. Susan had a badly fractured skull, two broken legs and a fractured pelvis. Her lungs had also been punctured by a number of broken ribs.

Weeks later, when she was conscious, she told me that she had seen her grandmother Alice walk up to her. She had taken hold of her hand and they had walked together in a beautiful garden where the flowers were large and vibrant. Alice had explained to Susan that she could stay for a short while but then she would have to leave. She told her that she would be safe and would return to full health, but one day they would meet again.

On another occasion, we had grouped together once more for a night of communication. Again John's spirit guide joined the circle to offer encouragement to all the developing mediums. Suddenly John began swaying to and fro. I became aware that a spirit person other than his guide had entered our circle. It was a male spirit. He started speaking through John. He said that he was a sailor and seemed to be in a very distressed state, depressed because he had lost his money and his livelihood.

I asked him if he knew that he had passed over to the world of spirit. He replied that he didn't know, but that he had visited his house recently and been extremely upset to find his wife and family totally ignoring him. They hadn't seemed to notice that he had arrived home.

I continued to question him about what he could remember. He informed me that he had decided to go on a trip for the day and had bought a ticket to the Isle of Man. He had boarded the ferry and gone down to the public bar for a drink. He had consumed a few drinks and then become very distressed over his finances and the fact that he had lost his job as a cabin steward on the ship he had worked on for the past 11 years. He had been frightened to go home and tell his wife, as he felt that she would be very angry. Also, he couldn't believe that a court case had gone badly wrong for him the previous day. He had expected a sizeable amount of money to be awarded to him, but now he was faced with legal fees amounting to many thousands of pounds. With no job and therefore no salary, he had no hope of being able to pay them. It was all too much for him.

I asked him why he had decided to board the Isle of Man ferry and he told me that he had planned to throw himself overboard. Then he said, 'Oh God! I *did* throw myself over! It didn't hurt, though! It was like going into a deep sleep.'

I told him that we could help him to go to the light, where he would be received by other members of his family in spirit, and with his agreement we successfully assisted him in reaching the heavenly light of the spirit realm. He would go in to a state of sleep and restoration there before taking his true place in the world of spirit. All of us in the circle were overjoyed that we had been able to help this poor man.

A few days later I received a shocking telephone call from my mother. She told me that a friend of my aunt's had gone missing from the Isle of Man ferry. No body had been found, but they had found a pile of neatly folded clothing, together with a watch, a ring and some money wrapped up in a towel, hidden behind one of the lifebelts. The man had been known to everyone as 'Percy'. My mother informed me that he had been a really nice man who had spent his life at sea working as a steward but had recently lost his job.

I was shocked! I told my mother the events that had occurred in my circle.

'D'you think it was Percy?' she whispered.

To this day the authorities have still not found

Percy's body, but we know exactly where he is – safe in the world of spirit.

There were many, many occasions when I experienced wonderful demonstrations of spirit communication whilst sitting in the circle with other mediums and occasionally I would be called upon by the spirit world to be used as a channel for them.

One evening, when we were settling into our seats to begin our meditation, I began to experience an amazing amount of mental imagery. I seemed to be walking along a pavement when suddenly I was felt an irre-sistible urge to look down at my feet. I could not believe what I was seeing. I was looking down at a pavement which was full of gold stars with famous names inscribed upon them – Greta Garbo, Cary Grant, Marilyn Monroe, John Wayne – they went on and on and on. I had the impression that a man was approach-ing me. I could not believe my eyes! He looked like Tony Curtis and he was asking me for a cigarette. I was vaguely wondering why somebody like Tony Curtis would be approaching me and asking me for a cigarette when I became aware once more of my surroundings and the people in the room. I remarked to the head of the circle that I had just had the oddest experience.

The head medium had begun giving messages to different members of the circle. When it was my turn to receive a message, he told me that his guides and inspirers were telling him that quite soon I would receive an invitation. This would come out of the blue. I would have to travel a great distance by aeroplane to a country which would allow me to stand up and demonstrate my mediumship. I asked for more details. The medium's guide said Hollywood Boulevard was just the right setting for people to sit up and take notice. This was just too much to hope for. Here I was, a medium who had only demonstrated in Spiritualist churches and conducted private sittings for people. Now I was being informed that I would travel to Hollywood. I was confused!

I asked once more whether a little more information could be afforded to me and also for the identity of the communicating spirit. I was informed that he was the person who had taken me to the pavement to show me the stars a few moments earlier. His name was Michael and he needed to come back to tell people close to him that he was doing well in the world of spirit. There the message ceased. No more information was forthcoming. I left the circle later that evening feeling more than a little bemused.

Three days later I received a letter from a friend named Geoff, who was an established medium, telling me that he had agreed to take a trip to California. He told me that if I could afford the airfare, I could accompany him. I immediately thought of the message I had received in the circle and wondered whether this could be what Michael had been talking about. Unfortunately, my finances did not allow me to accompany Geoff on his journey to California, but I asked him to call me upon his return.

Geoff returned from America couple of weeks later and we met up for lunch in Liverpool. He informed me that he had received an opportunity to demonstrate his mediumistic gifts whilst visiting the country and had been very well received. He showed me photographs of himself with the people he had met in California.

I commented that it looked as though he had had a wonderful time. 'Oh I did, Derek!' he replied.

After lunch had finished, we parted company and I returned to my office feeling slightly disappointed that I had not been able to afford the trip.

Time went by and I continued within the development circle. After a year or two, it disbanded, as we had all begun to go our separate ways, following our own different destinies. By now I had almost forgotten the message I had received from Michael.

In January 1999 I was fortunate enough to be invited to Los Angeles to take part in investigations with the International Society for Paranormal Research. During April of that year the ISPR visited the UK for the filming of *Ghosts of England* and *Ghosts of Belgrave Hall*. The results of these investigations are documented in my books *The Psychic World of Derek Acorah* and *The Psychic Adventures of Derek Acorah*.

The following July, I was invited once more to Los Angeles for the premiere of the two programmes, which would be held at the Vogue Theatre on Hollywood Boulevard.

Gwen and I arrived at LAX International Airport and were met by Dr Larry Montz of the ISPR. After we had had a good night's sleep he took us to the theatre to prepare for the evening showing of the two programmes.

Hollywood Boulevard is a busy street with restricted parking. After depositing Dr Montz's vehicle at a parking lot, we proceeded to walk to the theatre. As we turned the corner onto the famous boulevard I happened to look down at my feet. There they were: the famous names Greta Garbo, Cary Grant, Marilyn Monroe and John Wayne! I looked up and to my surprise could see, not ten yards in front of me, a person who was very much of this world and looked like Tony Curtis! Curiously, he was in evening dress, but sported a pair of very white training shoes. Memories of the evening long ago in the mediums' circle came flooding back. As I neared the man I waited with bated breath. Sure enough, as I drew adjacent to him he politely asked me whether I could spare a cigarette. I laughed as I handed him the packet and told him that I had thought that he was the great Tony Curtis. He smiled as he told me that he had worked as Tony's double on many of his films but now he was reduced to promoting sight-seeing tours of Hollywood. When he had first arrived in Hollywood with stars in his eyes he had thought that he would be a great actor and that the streets were paved with gold. 'Not so, young man,' he stated in a perfect English accent. 'Like many people, my dreams have turned to dust!'

I left the man, sadly reflecting that many people must have had his experience. I also wondered what on earth the connection was with the name of 'Michael' in spirit given years ago in Liverpool.

'Tonight,' Sam told me, 'you will receive the answer to your question.'

The time for the showing of *Ghosts of England* and *Ghosts of Belgrave Hall* arrived. The auditorium of the old theatre was full to bursting point.

Following the two films, together with the rest of the ISPR team, I went up on stage to speak to the audience about the filming and our experiences whilst doing so. The questions came thick and fast. As I was replying to one young lady, I suddenly became aware of a spirit man walking onto the stage from the wings. I recognized him instantly: it was Michael Landon. I was astounded! I had long been a fan of his since the days of *Bonanza*, when he played the character of Little Joe, and later when he starred in the programme *Little House on the Prairie*.

'I'm here to speak to my daughter Cheryl,' said Michael in his soft American drawl. 'It's most important.'

The young lady to whom I was speaking shrieked in surprise, 'Oh, my God! Please go on. I've been waiting for this for years!'

I imparted the information given by her father Michael. It was a message full of encouragement and love. I knew as I spoke that this was a time in her life when she needed to hear her father's words. As Michael faded he murmured to me that he would visit me once more when I was back at home in England.

After the question-and-answer session had been completed, Cheryl approached me. 'I need a little more information,' she said, 'as I have a very important decision to make. I know that you're leaving the States to go home early tomorrow. Could I please telephone you at your home?'

I agreed that she could telephone me when I had arrived back in the UK. The telephone call took place and from the content of the messages, I knew that it had been imperative that I acted as communicator between Cheryl in this world and her father in spirit. The message I had received in the circle so long ago had finally come true.

Table Tilting

This is also a form of communication used by the spirit world. Just like the ouija board, its origins lie in the parlour games of the Victorian era, which closely followed 'the ghost story which started Spiritualism' – the story being that of Margaret and Kate Fox, daughters of a poor farmer of Hydeville in Wayne County, New York State. The sisters claimed that they were able to communicate with spirits by means of a series of knocks. These reports have become famous as 'the Hydeville knockings'.

With table tilting, the people taking part either sit or

stand around a table with their fingertips gently touching the table's surface. As when using a ouija board, the spokesperson of the group, usually the presiding medium, requests any spirit present to make themselves known to the group by tilting or moving the table. There is usually no particular system or rhythm to the table's movement – the movement is merely an indication that a spirit entity is present and is wishing to interact with the people taking part.

If you are intending to experiment with this method of spirit communication, the best type of table to use is one of card-table dimensions but heavier construction. It is preferable to use a table with four legs rather than the central pedestal variety and the legs must be checked thoroughly beforehand for stability. Using a table with unsteady legs will give a false indication and will prove nothing in an investigation.

Some people prefer to attach a bell to the table, either fixed to the under-surface or hanging from a central pole, so that even the most minimal movement of the table will be registered by the ringing of the bell.

Anybody taking part in a table-tilting experiment must have complete faith in the other people around the table. It is simple for somebody to start pushing the table in order to start off the momentum, but this is a ludicrous thing to do. It does nothing more than waste everybody's time.

I have been present at table-tilting sessions when nothing whatsoever has happened with regard to movement, even though I have been very much aware that there was a spirit or spirits present. There have also been other occasions when the spirit people have been more than willing to take part and have vigorously moved the table not only in a tilting movement, but also around the room, with it ending up some feet from its original location.

Once I was fortunate to be heading a table-tilting experiment that took place in the home of a friend who also happened to be a medium. There were five sitters – two men and three women. We all made ourselves comfortable and placed the tips of our fingers on the edge of the tabletop. I offered up a prayer of invocation and enquired if there was anyone from the spirit world in attendance. If so, I asked them to step forward and make themselves known. There was no immediate reaction from the table, but there was a chilling of the room's temperature. I enquired whether this was the result of spiritual presence, but there was no answer. The atmosphere was very quiet and still.

After a few moments all the people present heard a knocking noise which sounded as though it came from beneath the table. At this point there was no detectable movement from the table. I asked once more whether there was a spirit person present. In response a loud knock was heard, this time coming from the top of the table.

I asked whether the spirit was female, but there was no response. I asked whether the spirit presence was male and we were immediately rewarded by the table seeming to lift and jolt. Once more I spoke out, thanking the male spirit for communicating with us. I continued by asking whether he would be prepared to answer some questions. Two large knocks on the top of the table were heard.

'Sir, did you die peacefully? Knock once for "yes" and twice for "no",' I said. Two loud knocks came in response followed by the table jolting almost uncontrollably for 15 to 20 seconds. The atmosphere in the room was charged. I then asked the spirit man whether his passing had been a long time ago. There was no response. I asked whether his passing had been within the last 10 years or so. The table jiggled and jumped around. I began to feel as though I was choking. I felt as though somebody had something around my neck and was pulling it tightly.

As I sat trying to keep my fingertips on the table, I heard Sam's voice. 'This is Peter,' he told me. 'He had a terrible accident at work.'

Before Sam could continue, the table seemed to take on a life of its own. At one point the edge lifted to almost under my neck and jaw. Gradually it calmed down again, allowing Sam to carry on. Apparently Peter had worked on the docks at Liverpool. One day the end of a rope attached to a winch had somehow got caught around his neck. The speed that the winch was travelling left no time for anybody to help Peter. He was strangled and his neck was broken.

I explained to him that we would like to help him achieve his proper destination in the world of spirit. I told him not to be afraid, that he would be met and taken to a place where his loved ones would be waiting for him. The table rocked slightly in response.

I asked the rest of the people with me to join me in sending out thoughts of love for Peter. As we did so, the most beautiful fragrance of flowers engulfed the room. I became aware of a lady in spirit who had been sent to collect Peter and to guide him to his rightful place in the spirit realm. As the fragrance faded, an atmosphere of peace and well-being pervaded the room. We all knew that Peter was safe with his family on the heavenly side of life.

Dowsing Rods and Pendulums

The use of dowsing rods and pendulums has already been explained *(see page 7)*. As mentioned earlier, not all investigators use dowsing rods or pendulums, and I do not use them myself, but I have been with other mediums when they have been using a pendulum and have witnessed it spinning wildly as it detects spirit presence. I have also been present when dowsing rods have swung and crossed as they have detected water sources and ley lines.

I do not particularly advocate the use of pendulums or dowsing rods when investigating spirit activity, but I know that some people do value their results and they can add an interesting element to a paranormal investigation.

Invisible Friends

Many are the stories I have received from people complaining that their child has an 'invisible friend'. This is not easy to deal with, as family life always has to be broadened to encompass the 'friend' – an extra table setting, an extra chair, the cry of 'Watch out! You're sitting on my friend!' All very inconvenient!

The fact remains, though, that generally the children who claim friendship with someone their parents cannot see are very psychic. Their friends are spirit people – unseen by their parents, but nonetheless real. The friend may also be an animal, usually a small dog or a cat. A friend of my own had a son who was friends with a doggie spirit he called Muffin. His parent's lives were ruled for a number of years by this little dog, but eventually, when the boy was about ten years of age, he talked less and less of Muffin and eventually the dog disappeared back to the spirit realms.

I recall another child, Kirsty, who was the daughter of a woman called Rhona, who used to visit me regularly for sittings at my office in Liverpool. Kirsty had talked of her friend Betsy from almost the day that she had learned to speak. Whenever Rhona asked Kirsty to do anything, the child would always reply: 'I'll have to ask Betsy whether she thinks it's OK!' Rhona was at the end of her tether until the day Kirsty started telling her what Betsy had said about different events taking place within the family. Apparently Betsy would make predictions and they would come true! Fascinated by this situation, and with the idea that she had her own personal psychic on tap, Rhona began to encourage her daughter to converse with Betsy and to ask her opinion about certain situations. At this stage Kirsty was still only about 12 years of age.

Rhona called me up regularly with updates on what Kirsty had been able to tell her via Betsy and I tried to convince her that what she was doing was wrong. I told her that although she should be sympathetic and listen to her daughter when she spoke about Betsy, she should not be encouraging her to ask questions of the spirit world. It was far too great an undertaking for a child of her tender years. Nevertheless, Rhona continued, and even took to inviting friends round so that they too could benefit from what Betsy had to say.

Finally, she made an appointment to see me and asked whether she could bring Kirsty along. I agreed, but wondered why on earth she was bringing the child.

As soon as I opened my office door, however, I understood. The last time I had seen Kirsty had been about 18 months earlier. She had been an active child, bright and intelligent, with a great zest for life. I hardly recognized the quiet and morose young person who stood in front of me now.

'I don't know what's happening,' Rhona blurted out. 'Kirsty's become very withdrawn and doesn't want to go out with her friends. All she does is stay in her bedroom all the time. I've taken her to the doctor and he says there's nothing wrong with her physically.'

I was immediately aware that poor Kirsty was drained of all her psychic energies. Her mother's eagerness to take advantage of the gifts her daughter possessed was taking too great a toll on the girl. What she needed was to cut off from the world of spirit – to allow Betsy to recede back into that world in the manner of all childhood 'invisible friends'.

I took Kirsty to one side on the pretext of helping me to carry cups of coffee. She confided to me that she did not want to talk to Betsy any more but felt that she had to because her mother was encouraging her to do so. If Rhona or one of her friends had a problem, they would ask Kirsty to ask Betsy to give them an insight into how it might be solved. But the poor child felt so pressurized by the responsibilities being heaped upon her.

'And not only that, Derek, but Betsy doesn't come to me as much now, so I have to just guess at the answers! I'm afraid that I'll get everything wrong and it'll cause trouble for Mum.'

Kirsty also told me that she felt shunned by her friends, as they called her 'weird' and 'a spook' because it had got around the neighbourhood that she was psychic. This was the reason why she stayed in her bedroom and did not want to socialize with people of her own age.

What was happening to Kirsty was what happens to all psychic children with invisible friends. As the host child grows towards puberty, their visitors go back to the world of spirit. No doubt they will reappear in later life as guardians or door keepers, or maybe even as main spirit guides, but the spirit world knows that such burdens are not to be heaped upon the shoulders of a youngster just setting out on the pathway to adult life.

I felt very sorry for Kirsty. As a child I too had glimpsed the world of spirit, but I had had the comfort of turning to my grandmother, who could explain to me the reasons for my experiences. I had been allowed to grow without the burden of having to worry about any work that I might do with the world of spirit in later life. In short, I had been allowed to follow my childhood dreams and develop my psychic abilities naturally when the time was right for me.

Kirsty and I returned to the room where Rhona was sitting. I explained Kirsty's fears to her and told her in no uncertain terms that it was wrong to burden her daughter with having to 'come across with the goods' psychically at such a young age and that she was being drained both psychically and physically by the pressure that she was being placed under. I advised her that at some time in the future Kirsty might wish to use her gifts, but that it should be left up to her to decide. We all have free will, but if something is meant to happen, it will. I used my own experiences as an example. When I was a child, I had shunned the idea of working with the world of spirit, but my life had evolved in such a way that I was led onto the pathway.

Rhona was full of remorse. 'I wish I'd listened to you, Derek,' she told me, 'but it was so exciting to be able to ask Kirsty something and have Betsy come up with the answer.'

Mother and daughter walked away from my office that day with fresh understanding. Kirsty felt relieved that she would no longer be expected to sit with adults and give them readings and Rhona understood that her daughter had to be allowed to be a teenager and not be placed in the unnatural position of having to take on the woes of the adult world.

Twelve months later Rhona contacted me once more. 'I'd like to come to you for a reading, Derek. It's over a year since I had one. When can you book me in?'

Scrying

Scrying is yet another method used to connect with members of the spirit world. A reflective surface is used, either a bowl of water or a mirror or a crystal ball. The aim is to see a spirit form in the reflection of the water or mirror or in the depths of the crystal ball.

If you are attempting this method of spirit connection, you should sit comfortably in front of the reflective surface. Empty your mind of all thoughts and stare deeply, but not fixedly, at your own reflection. After a few moments your vision will blur and your face will disappear, to be replaced by that of a person in spirit. The details of the room you are sitting in may also change to the interior of a room familiar to the spirit person you have made contact with.

In my days of private readings at my office in Liverpool I was often asked to use the crystal ball. I recall one particular lady who had arranged to travel from Dublin to see me. On the day of her reading she telephoned me from Dublin airport to inform me that her plane had been cancelled but that she would catch the next flight to Liverpool some two hours later. I told her not to worry but to come straight into the city centre after landing at the airport. I was therefore left with some time on my hands. I decided that this would be an ideal opportunity to answer some letters.

I had just started to open my post when the doorbell rang. I went down the stairs to open the main door of the building. On the doorstep stood a lady who told me that she was in Liverpool for the day and had decided that rather than telephoning me, she would simply call by to see whether I had a cancellation. She introduced herself as Irene and told me that she knew my waiting list was long, but she was wondering whether there was any possibility of seeing me that day.

Irene seemed very anxious. I also felt that she was not in the best of health. I told her it did not often happen, but I did have a couple of spare hours and if she wished I would conduct a sitting for her there and then. She could not believe her luck, as at that time my waiting list was some seven or eight months. We went upstairs and I prepared myself to see what I could do to help Irene.

Irene sat down and looked around my office. She told me that it was not at all as she had imagined and added that she felt quite comfortable in the surroundings. Apparently she had imagined all sorts of pictures of witches and warlocks, dark hangings and the smell of incense. I laughed and told her that all I required was the presence of my spirit guide, Sam.

'I've one question to ask, Derek,' Irene said. 'Would you mind using the crystal ball with me? My mum used to visit a local medium and she always used a crystal ball and was amazingly accurate!'

I asked Irene to take the large crystal ball on my desk from its stand and hold it for a while. We sat in silence for a while as Irene held the ball and I opened myself up to the world of spirit.

I took the ball from Irene's hands and stared into it. I was surprised by the first image that I received: I saw myself walking down a corridor. I sensed that there was the smell of anaesthetic in the air. It was a hospital corridor. Then I saw Irene come into the picture. She entered a room, sat down and started talking to a man in a grey suit. I saw her suddenly put her head in her hands. I related the information I was receiving to her and asked her whether she understood why I was seeing this. She told me that yes, she could understand why.

I looked once again into the crystal. I was impressed with the name 'Patterson'. Irene looked excited and asked me to carry on. From the cloudy images of the hospital scene there appeared a lady who was smiling broadly. I described her to Irene and told her that I was being impressed to say the name 'Anne Marie'. I knew that Anne Marie was watching over Irene from the higher side of life. In fact I quickly gained the impression that she was Irene's mother. I asked her whether this was the case. With tears in her eyes, Irene confirmed that this was indeed her mother, who had suffered from cancer before being taken over to the world of spirit.

As I gazed down at the smiling face of Anne Marie, the image of a dog appeared – a black and white spaniel. Irene was really sobbing by this time. The dog had been her pet for nearly nine years before he had passed over to spirit only seven months previously. I received the name 'Abbie'.

'That was my dog's name,' whispered Irene.

Now the crystal seemed to cloud over. What appeared next was something I had not expected at all. I seemed to go into the crystal, then suddenly I was looking at people who were dressed in green clothing with green masks across their faces. I realized that I had been taken into an operating theatre and that the man leaning over a woman on the operating table was a doctor. I looked more closely and realized that the woman was Irene! I could hear a discussion regarding the surgery the doctor was performing. 'She has a tumour,' he said.

Then I saw Anne Marie walk over to the operating table. She placed her hand on Irene's forehead. I could hear her words: 'You'll be OK, love! You won't be joining me just yet!'

I felt a total feeling of reassurance from just hearing this alone. I was suddenly rushed back to normal consciousness and, with great sensitivity, told Irene what I had just experienced.

She was very calm. 'Derek, you just wouldn't know how correct you are,' she said.

I concentrated on the crystal ball once more. I could see a date: 5 February. I knew that all would be well by that time.

As I gave Irene the information I was receiving, I was suddenly aware of a spirit lady building up in the office beside her. It was Anne Marie. She thanked me for passing on the information to Irene and for giving her the confidence to go ahead with the operation that she needed. She told me that Irene was aware of her medical situation – that was why I had felt comfortable enough to relay the details to her.

As I concentrated once more on the crystal ball I became aware of Irene being taken to a room that was obviously a recovery room. A nurse was in attendance. Then the picture changed. I was shown a different environment. It was a cosy living room. Irene was sitting on a sofa reading. The telephone rang and Irene went to answer it. I could not hear the conversation, but I could tell by the wide smile on Irene's face and her gasp of joy that it was good news. I then heard the words 'All clear!' The date 5 February appeared once more in the crystal ball.

Irene thanked me for the information I had given her. She asked me to pass on her love to her mother. 'I don't have to,' I told her. 'She can hear you for herself.'

One of the telephone calls I received on the following 5 February was from Irene. 'You were right,' she told me. 'I've just received news from the hospital that my operation was a complete success and that the tumour was benign.'

Automatic Writing

Automatic writing is yet another form of spirit communication. It is practised mainly by mediums, but of course there is nothing to prevent anybody from attempting to contact the spirit world in this manner. I would stress, however, that in my opinion, as with any other method of contacting spirit, a prayer of protection be uttered prior to any such attempt taking place. You should request that only the highest and the best of communicants gets in touch with you.

Not everyone will be successful at automatic writing and much perseverance may be necessary. Even then, success is not guaranteed. However, you might like to give it a try.

You will need to sit at a table on a comfortable chair. There should be no distractions around you and if possible you should be alone. If there are other people in the room with you they should remain absolutely still and quiet and must not cause a disruption or diversion.

You should place a pad of plain paper in front of you and take a pen or pencil in your hand, holding it loosely in a relaxed manner between your thumb and forefinger. Place it lightly upon the top sheet of paper. Empty your mind of all conscious thought and let the pen or pencil move freely across the paper. Do not attempt to direct its movement, but let it flow naturally in whatever direction it chooses. Do not attempt to read or concentrate on what is being written, just close your mind to the words or images which appear. The whole point of the exercise is to ensure that what appears on the sheet of paper in front of you is received from a spirit entity and is not the product of your own consciousness.

After a period of perhaps 20 to 30 minutes has elapsed, put the pen down and look at what you have achieved. The fortunate among you may find that words or names pertaining to the property you are investigating have been written on the sheets of paper. If there is any information that you do not recognize as relating to the location, do not dismiss it immediately but go away and research it. Too many times to recall I have received information through automatic writing which has been dismissed, only to hear at a later date, as a result of further research, that it was indeed correct.

The Tarot

Almost as fascinating and mysterious as the Tarot cards themselves is their lack of proven origin. Many authorities have written extensively about the subject and many interesting theories have been put forward, but we are still no nearer knowing for certain just where those origins lie. One theory suggests that the Tarot originated in China, where playing cards were used before the eleventh century AD; alternatively India is a possible birthplace. The first documented appearance of the cards in Europe can be traced to 1392, when an entry was made in the court ledger of King Charles VI of France for three packs of illustrated cards. At this time Christianity reigned supreme and it was hundreds of years later, in the eighteenth century, that certain French occultists claimed that the Tarot originated in Egypt. In the nineteenth century it was noted that there was an apparent link between the 22 letters of the Hebrew alphabet which were said to connect with the 22 paths of the cabalistic Tree of Life. The mystery is ongoing.

The Tarot is made up of 78 cards – 56 Minor Arcana cards which are divided into four suits rather like modern playing cards, and 22 Major Arcana cards which have unusual names such as 'The Fool', 'The Hierophant', 'The Hanged Man', etc. How the cards work is unknown, though it has been suggested that the answer lies within the mind of the enquirer rather than in the actual cards, which act as a bridge between the conscious and unconscious knowledge.

Many, many decks of Tarot cards have been designed and produced, some of which are beautiful works of art. In years gone by when I would conduct personal readings, I would use the Rider-Waite pack.

In those long-gone days I found that people could not quite accept the fact that I was capable of giving them information about their lives without the aid of something tangible that they could see. In those early days, spirit communication was not so readily acceptable. People viewed spirit guides as something rather spooky and as the province of 'gooks' who sat in darkened rooms 'trying to conjure up dead people'. If there was a crystal ball, or even better, a deck of Tarot cards in use, it appeared that my clients accepted my gifts more easily. I would ask them whether they required the cards and invariably the answer would be: 'Yes please!' What they did not realize was that I was communicating with Sam, together with my other guides and helpers, in order to help them with their questions or communicate with their loved ones in the spirit world.

I also had another companion with me in those days. My German Shepherd dog Cara was only young at that time, but she was used to accompanying me to my office and would spend her days lying at my feet under the desk. She became something of a celebrity walking through the city centre before the day's work. When we reached the office each day, as soon as I lifted the box containing my Tarot cards, Cara would scuttle under the desk and go to sleep. I don't think that people were always aware that she was there and that she was privy to the intimate details of their lives.

I recall one lady named Cath who visited me. She walked into my office and smiled as she took a seat opposite me. I asked her whether she would like a sitting using just my mediumship or whether she would like me to incorporate the Tarot in her reading.

'Oooh! Use the cards, luv!' she told me. 'I don't go with all this talking to the dead stuff!'

I smiled as I shuffled the cards. There was a sharp intake of breath from Cath as I dealt out Death.

'Don't worry,' I told her. 'The Death card does not indicate the passing of somebody to spirit. It merely tells me that somebody around you faces a new beginning in their life.'

I conducted Cath's reading. I was fortunate in that her mother and father in spirit were willing to communicate with me. They asked me to pass on their love to her and gave messages of hope regarding her husband's redundancy. 'Tell her not to worry,' whispered the Cath's mother. 'Jim'll have a new job before the month is out.'

The reading continued in the same upbeat manner. I was pleased to see that there was nothing untoward being brought onto Cath's pathway, as judging from the trials she had had to undergo in the past, she really deserved the good things which lay in front of her.

As Cath's reading drew to a close, her mother and father having receded back to the world of spirit, a shuffling noise could be heard coming from under the desk.

'What's that?' asked Cath nervously.

'It's my dog Cara,' I told her. 'She spends her days here with me, but don't worry because she's very well behaved!'

Cath stood up and picked up the shopping bag that had been at her feet throughout her reading. As she brought the bag up onto the desk, a paper bag fell out with the remnants of a beefburger hanging out of it. Unknown to either Cath or me, Cara had been helping herself to that night's dinner!

I apologized profusely and gave Cath the money to purchase more food for the evening meal.

Fortunately she had a sense of humour. 'The Tarot cards didn't tell you about that, did they, Derek?' she laughed.

CHAPTER 7

Haunted Hotels

There are numerous allegedly haunted hotels through-out the United Kingdom, many of which readily open their doors in welcome to ghost-hunting groups and paranormal investigators.

I have stayed in countless establishments where I have shared my room with members of the spirit world, but I have to say that neither Gwen nor I have ever been kept from our slumbers by spirit activity. When settling down for the night I have been aware of the movement of spirit people around the room – maybe the creak of the floorboards as they walk across the floor, the click or rap on a surface as they potter around their old familiar home or workplace, or the whispering as they chat – but I have never been disturbed by flying objects or moving furniture.

The Bull

I recall staying at the Bull in Long Melford, Suffolk, during the filming of the LIVINGtv programme *Antiques Ghost Show*. Gwen and I, accompanied by genealogist Anthony Adolph, had driven from

Canterbury where the initial filming had taken place. It was late at night, but we were all charmed on reaching the hotel to see that our accommodation for the next few nights was an old black and white inn.

The Bull Hotel was a beautiful old building. I was told by the staff that although it had originally been built as a private dwelling in 1450 by a local wool merchant, after the first hundred years it had become an inn and had remained so ever since.

I knew immediately upon entering the old building that there would be spirit activity within its mellow walls and I was particularly drawn to the lounge, which housed a massive fireplace and also a liberal amount of honey-coloured timber beams. I also felt that there was a lot of spirit activity in the hallway which ran between the stairs and the dining room and passed in front of the reception desk.

My days were taken up with the filming of the programme, but during the evening I was able to relax and soak up the atmosphere of the old inn. Standing in front of the fire in the lounge, which was empty of other residents at the time, I opened myself up to the vibrations of the spirit world.

I was shown a man in spirit in seventeenth-century dress. He did not communicate with me, nor did Sam give me his name. I observed his movements as he pottered around the room, eventually settling himself in a chair. He did not appear particularly agitated or uneasy, but seemed to be waiting for somebody. After a while his form faded and I was left on my own with only the crackling of the open fire to keep me company.

At this point Gwen entered the lounge, followed closely by Anthony and Chris Gower, the antiques expert for the programme. Their chattering soon dispelled any mystical atmosphere remaining in the room.

Later, on my way out of the lounge, as I passed the reception desk I asked the lady in attendance, whom I will call Carole, whether anybody had reported seeing anything unusual in the lounge. She informed me that she had heard a story that in 1648 Richard Everard had been murdered in the hallway as a result of an argument with a man named Roger Greene. She said that his body had been laid out in the hotel but that it had vanished overnight. Now it was alleged that his ghost walked the hallway. I realized this must have been the spirit man I had seen.

I thanked her and added that I was also drawn to a door at the end of the hallway leading to the dining room.

'Oh, that often opens and closes by itself,' she laughed. 'I've often wondered whether it's the ghost of Everard doing that!'

Carole went on to tell me that before she began working at the hotel she had heard a rumour that poltergeist activity had been experienced by a previous owner, Col. Dawson, and his staff. Apparently one of the waiters had had the unnerving experience of having a copper jug thrown at him by an invisible force. The chairs in the dining room had been seen moving around on their own and the sound of breaking crockery had been heard by guests, though Carole herself had not witnessed any of these phenomena and did not know of any similar reports from the present staff.

I thanked Carole and joined Gwen, Anthony and Chris for dinner. I was not at the hotel to conduct an investigation, after all. It was merely idle curiosity and my experience in the lounge that had prompted me to ask. Normally, of course, if I were conducting an investigation for a programme such as *Most Haunted* I would not be willing to talk about a building's history with anybody.

After dinner Gwen and I retired to our bedroom. It was a comfortable room overlooking the front car park of the hotel. When I had entered the room earlier in the day to drop off our luggage, shower and change, I had not noticed much about it, but as I sat in the easy chair there at the end of the day I knew that we would experience spirit activity during our stay there.

I asked Gwen whether she could feel anything in the atmosphere, but she shook her head. 'No! But you know that I'm about as psychic as that!' she said, rapping her knuckles on a table.

If I have ever told Gwen that I can sense that there will be spirit activity in a room she has made a practice of leaving a camera on the bedside cabinet and has asked me to wake her should I sense anything of a paranormal nature taking place. This allows her to take photographs in an effort to capture paranormal activity on camera.

At the Bull we had turned out the lights and I was lying in bed mulling over the day's events when I heard a shuffling noise in the corner of the room next to the bathroom door. Then I saw a young girl in spirit. She was dressed in a long floral print dress tied behind with a large bow and had long blonde hair hanging down to her waist but held back from her face by a broad ribbon. I whispered to Gwen, who picked up the camera and proceeded to photograph the area I indicated.

After that, each night the young girl would appear and each night Gwen would take photographs. The girl did not communicate with me, but she would often look at me and smile as she danced around. When we went back home and had the photographs developed, we were rewarded with many orbs on the images.

As well as the young girl, for the duration of our stay at the Bull I often saw the spirit man in the lounge and the hallway. I also saw brief images of many other spirit people throughout the old building, but curiously, given the horrific events which are alleged to have taken place there, I never felt uneasy or uncomfortable. The atmosphere of the inn was restful and at peace.

When I approached the reception desk as I was preparing to leave on the final day I mentioned to Carole that not only had I seen spirits in the hallway and the lounge, but I had also experienced spirit activity in my bedroom. She laughed as she told me that they had purposely allocated the haunted bedroom to me!

The Hare and Hounds

The Hare and Hounds in Westonbirt near Tetbury in Gloucestershire is another establishment where spirit activity in the bedroom was more than a little noticeable. Room 34 contained a spirit entity who insisted on turning the kettle on all the time. When he was not doing that he was turning the television off and on. Fortunately his activities did not continue through the night – he seemed to be happy enough merely shuffling around quietly during the dark hours.

The Castle and Ball Hotel

There is a hotel in the centre of Marlborough – the Castle and Ball Hotel. I had travelled through atrocious weather and was relieved to reach it. Yet again, just to make me feel at home, the management had arranged that my room would be the one that housed their 'resident ghost'.

The spirit chappie did not let anyone down! As soon as I walked into the room I saw him smiling cheerily at me whilst gesturing a welcome with a hand firmly clutching what I knew to be his favourite pipe. He even joined me in the bathroom and, whilst I showered, conversationally informed me that he had lived in the hotel for many years before he had passed to the spirit world. He still visited it from time to time just to make sure that everything was being run to his liking and that the guests were happy.

After I had finished in the bathroom, the spirit man, still puffing away on his pipe, accompanied me down the hallway to the cigarette machine. This was one person who would not tell me off for smoking!

The Blue Bell

The Blue Bell Hotel in Milnthorpe, Cumbria, is another hotel where I experienced spirit phenomena.

I arrived at the hotel on a summer Sunday afternoon. It was quiet and peaceful and as the afternoon drew to a close, the church bells rang out over the fields, drowning the lazy sound of bumblebees and the birds as they prepared to roost for the night.

I had ambled down the lane a short distance and was returning to the old inn when I became aware of two ladies in spirit. They were very elegantly dressed and both carried parasols in the early Victorian style. They seemed to be chatting quietly to one another as they strolled across the front of the inn. As I neared them I could see that they were quite elderly but seemed very much at peace with their surroundings and took no notice whatsoever of me. Sam was not conversing with me, so I had to be satisfied with my psychic deduction that the two ladies had been former residents of the inn.

I walked through the small glazed porch and on to the cocktail bar, and as I sat waiting to order tea, the whole scene changed. I felt as though I was drifting further back in time. I was in another room – rather shabby, with occasional tables laden with sheaves of paper and books. A huge desk stood in the corner, behind which sat a grey-haired man with his head bent over his writing. He wore a cleric's collar. I had the distinct feeling that I was in the presence of a priest or a vicar who was busy writing a sermon to deliver to his congregation. Once again, though I asked Sam to explain what I was seeing, he remained deaf to my pleas.

Then the scene shifted and changed once again. I felt that I had been catapulted forward in time. I felt that I was surrounded by children – far too many children for one family – yet I could detect no sense of teaching going on in the building. Still Sam did not come to my aid. I was therefore resigned to the fact that I would have to resort to a more earthly assistant when the waitress finally arrived with my tea.

When my tea arrived, I asked the lady who was serving me whether she knew the history of the building. She told me that she believed that the inn had been a vicarage between the fifteenth century and the mid-nineteenth century, when it had been purchased by two ladies, the Woods sisters. They had lived there until they had passed to the world of spirit. The house had then been used as a dormitory by a school, after which it had been bought by a Mr Hunter, who used it once more as a family home. After that, it had become an inn when Mr Hunter sold it to a Mr Dickinson.

The waitress told me that there were lots of stories attached to the inn which involved Bonnie Prince Charlie, who had been in nearby Kendal during his bid for the English throne. There was one tale which involved the church silver being hidden in a hole within the building.

I would have loved to have conducted an investigation at the Blue Bell Hotel. It would have been fascinating to unfold its rich history, with the help of Sam of course, who hopefully would have been a little more forthcoming with information and not have chosen to take the day off, as he had on that beautiful summer Sunday!

The *Queen Mary*

One of the more unusual hotels I have stayed in has to be the *Queen Mary*. Permanently docked at Long Beach, California, she still retains an air of thirties elegance redolent of the time when she was the largest ship in the world and the pride of the Cunard Line fleet.

The history of the ship is long and illustrious. She has carried some of the greatest Hollywood names – Marlene Dietrich, Fred Astaire, Clark Gable and Spencer Tracey to name but a few. She was visited and travelled upon frequently by royalty. During the Second World War, whilst she was painted camouflage grey, Sir Winston Churchill used her as his floating war office. She was dubbed 'the Grey Ghost', owing to her superior speed and manoeuvring tactics. Churchill said of her, 'Built for the arts of peace and to link the old world with the new, the *Queen Mary* challenges the fury of Hitlerism to defend the liberties of civilization.'

The *Queen Mary* was retired in 1967 and it did not take long for reports of ghostly goings-on to emerge. Ghostly sightings are now numerous and occur on all levels of the ship. There is the spectre of a young crewman who was crushed to death in 1966; in Sir Winston's Piano Bar a white lady makes her presence known; the hospital area and the morgue have had their fair share of sightings; and the kitchens, stairways, boiler room and swimming pools all play host to ghostly visitors.

The most heart-rending ghostly memory played out from time to time on board the *Queen Mary* is of a time in 1942 when the Grey Ghost accidentally struck her escort cruiser, HMS *Curacoa*, slicing her in half. Three hundred men perished on that day. At the site of the collision in the ship's bows, shouting voices and pounding noises have been heard.

During my stay on the *Queen Mary* I was frequently surprised on entering my cabin to find an industrious ghostly cabin steward going about his chores, cleaning and tidying up just as he had in the days when the *Queen Mary* was *the* mode of travel for those who wished to cross the Atlantic in style.

Whilst walking the promenade deck early one morning looking out across the sunlit waters towards Long Beach, I became aware that I was not alone. A little further along the covered deck, staring out towards the town in exactly the same manner, stood a spirit lady. She was smartly though inexpensively dressed and looked to me to be in her early twenties. As she gazed out across the waters, I felt that she was not viewing the quiet lapping of the Long Beach dock but the rolling waves of the Atlantic. I also had the distinct feeling that we were no longer static but were travelling at some speed away from English shores. I was clairvoyantly shown a picture of the Statue of Liberty, the huge edifice which guards the entrance to New York harbour.

'This is Margaret,' Sam whispered to me. 'She was on her journey to make a new life in America with her husband, whom she had met and married whilst he was in England. The *Queen Mary* brought her and many other GI brides to the US to be reunited with her husband. Unfortunately, when Margaret arrived she found no one waiting for her – she had been abandoned. She brought herself over to the spirit world as a result.'

I felt so sad for the young lady who had no doubt boarded this marvellous ship with such enthusiasm and hope. She had been dreaming of a new life with a new husband. Those hopes had been dashed by the callous person she had attached herself to. I wondered why she would be visiting the *Queen Mary*. Sam supplied the answer: 'Because these are her last happy memories. Her last happy thoughts were leaning against the deck rail, looking out towards what she thought would be the beginning of a new life.'

No wonder the *Queen Mary* has an air of sadness about it. Amongst all the joyous experiences that have taken place on board I am sure that there are many other stories, just like Margaret's, that were not so happy.

Paddy McGinty's

Although I have entitled this chapter 'Haunted Hotels', I would like to add a small piece dealing with an investigation I carried out at the public house known as Paddy McGinty's in Ipswich. Paddy McGinty's is a typical pub, but it is home to a rather interesting story.

It was nearing Hallowe'en and I was close to Ipswich, having completed a theatre engagement in Felixstowe, when I was asked whether I would conduct an investigation of the old pub for a television programme.

As I entered the pub and looked around, at first I could see nothing of any particular interest. There was a bar and a seating area and lively music issued from the jukebox. The landlord welcomed me and showed me round. As we walked around I was aware that there was indeed a spirit presence who regularly visited the premises. He seemed to be a monk, rather a quiet soul whom I suppose some would consider sinister. However, I had the distinct impression that in spite of a horrific end, he was compassionate and would do no harm.

When I had completed my investigation, the landlord told me that his pub was opposite Christchurch

Mansion, which had been built on the site of the Holy Trinity Priory, which had been home to many monks up until the time of Henry VIII's dissolution of the monasteries. At that time the monastery had been ransacked and the monks escaped. However, one monk still remains. He is reputed to have been thrown down an indoor well.

The landlord told me that he felt that the monk had saved his life some time ago. He had warned him of an imminent fire, and because of the warning, the fire had been avoided.

So, if you want to go to Ipswich and visit Paddy McGinty's ghost, I recommend that you visit the hostelry in Northgate Street, Ipswich.

CHAPTER 8

Ghosts in the Workplace

You might not think that any spirit would wish to return to the place in which they had worked on this side of life. I can assure you, however, that this is indeed the case. From time to time I have been called to investigate strange goings-on in offices and factories and have discovered spirit activity.

A Building Society Office

Once I was called to investigate a building society office in Liverpool city centre by Christine, who was the manager of the branch. Staff members had been bothered by papers being inexplicably moved during the night when the office was closed. It was causing mayhem with the filing and making life rather difficult for everyone. The cleaners had been closely questioned, but they had denied moving anything. They had told Christine, however, that they had often felt as though someone unseen had been with them as they had gone about their duties during the evening.

The office was situated in one of the old buildings in the business part of Liverpool city centre. As I walked into what was now a modern and light open-planned interior, I was whooshed back in time to the sixties – the time when I would have just about been starting out in my footballing career. As I opened myself up to the spirit world I was taken back. The bright paint and light woodwork disappeared and I saw instead a tall ceiling with intricate plasterwork. The walls were panelled halfway up in dark wood. The higher part of the wall was painted in a dismal pale green colour. There was a high counter in the same dark wood as the panelling which ran the length of the room. At each end of this counter stood a type of half door which contained panes of stained glass. I was standing in what had once been a bank of the type I remembered from my boyhood. The brassware was burnished, and inkwells and blotters had been placed along the counter.

'Was this building once a bank?' I asked Christine.

She told me that it had indeed been a bank but that it had been bought by the building society in the early 1970s.

I walked around the room. As I did so, I became aware of a gentleman from the spirit world. He was rather large, with a florid complexion. His hair was sparse and grey. He wore a dark suit with a collar and tie and had a pair of dark-framed spectacles on his nose. 'A bank manager,' I thought to myself.

'No,' Sam told me. 'George was not a manager.'

The spirit man was not communicating with me directly. He was going about his business, leafing through papers on a desk which only I could see. It was not a desk constructed of stainless steel and plywood, but a heavy leather-topped one mounted on pillars of drawers. The top of the desk was covered in papers, which to me looked like share certificates.

'Mr Roberts dealt with bank customers' investments,' Sam said to me. 'He loved his stocks and shares!'

As I watched, the spirit of George Roberts busied himself with writing in a large ledger. He then suddenly looked to either side of him and started frantically searching through the papers on his desk. He looked in the drawers, appearing to open and close them more and more frantically as though he was looking for something he had misplaced.

The scene faded. I asked Sam what the relevance of it was.

'Poor George,' said Sam. 'He was dedicated to his work. One day some very important papers disappeared from his desk, and try as he might, he could not find them. He became more and more agitated and upset, and finally succumbed to a heart attack. He passed to spirit on that very spot. The missing papers were found the following day. They had been inadvertently picked up by somebody else in the office and placed in the wrong file.'

I now knew the reason for papers in the office being moved around. It was the spirit of George Roberts on his interminable quest for the missing documents.

I told Christine what I had seen. 'What a sad story,' she commented. 'Poor man! Is there anything you can do to help him?'

'Sam will bring him peace,' I told her. 'He will tell George that he need search no more – that the papers are safe and he can forget his torment.'

The next time I had reason to be in Liverpool city centre I called in to see Christine. I was pleased when she told me that everything seemed to have settled down in the office. George had obviously found peace at last.

Albert Dock

On another occasion I was asked to visit Albert Dock in Liverpool. For those readers who do not know, Albert Dock was once a group of the large warehouses which lined the banks of the river Mersey when Liverpool was a thriving port. They have now been redeveloped and are luxury apartments and shops.

I had been called in by Peter, who rented one of the shop units on the ground floor of Albert Dock. He had been hearing strange clanking and banging, but try as he might, he could not find the cause. He had paid for plumbers and electricians to come and check all the wiring and the pipework, but they could not find any trace of a fault which could be causing the noises.

I knew before I arrived at Peter's premises what I would find. The noises would merely be a replay of the dockside activity that had taken place when the warehouse had been used for the storage of cargo from the many ships which called into the port of Liverpool.

I had arranged to meet Peter at his unit after closing time. It was strange walking through the empty walkways which were usually thronged with shoppers and visitors to the dock. Across the square of water I could see the lights of the restaurants and I gazed briefly at the floating weather map, a relic of the days when ITV's *This Morning* programme was broadcast from the Albert Dock complex. I stopped to look at the plaque bearing the name of Jesse Hartley, architect and engineer of the original dock building. I felt some pride in the knowledge that this great man, a member of the famous jam and preserve manufacturing family, had been a cousin to my grandmother, the very same lady who had placed my feet firmly upon my spiritual pathway.

Peter was waiting for me. We sat down in his shop in silence. After a short while we began to hear first of all shufflings and then the noise of footsteps. They were accompanied by the rasping noise of ropes being dragged across a stone floor. There was also the clanking of chains banging metal against metal. It was just as I had thought – Peter was hearing the activity of dock workers as they went about their daily task of loading and unloading.

'You've nothing to worry about, Peter,' I said. 'It's all residual energy – noises from the past.'

'Thank goodness for that!' exclaimed Peter. 'I thought that I'd arrive in one day to find my stock damaged by water because of leaking pipes, or even worse, the whole place going up in smoke because of faulty wiring!'

I told Peter that he needn't worry. The reason why he was aware of all the noise was that he tended to stay later than all the other shopkeepers and when everywhere was empty and quiet, he would obviously be more able to hear the noises of times gone by.

An Old Mill

The Albert Dock is not the only place where I have caught a glimpse of the working environment of many years ago.

Whilst working on the television programme *Predictions with Derek Acorah* for Granada Breeze, I was taken to investigate an old mill just outside Manchester city centre. The building stood on the banks of the Manchester ship canal. Production of cloth had ceased many years ago and one of the floors of the building had been used more recently in the production of stage scenery, although that too had now ceased, the company having moved to different premises. The producer of *Predictions with Derek Acorah* had heard from one of the stage scenery staff that the floor where they had worked was haunted. It seemed a good place to film an investigation.

We were met outside the huge old building by the carctaker, Chris, a man in his sixties. He led us up the precarious staircase to the first floor and showed us around the part of the building which was still safe, then stood back hopefully as the cameras rolled and I began to open myself up to the spirit world.

The picture that unfolded before my clairvoyant eyes was one of frantic activity. Hands and shuttles flew in the constant production of cloth. There were men, women and small children crammed into the area, all intent on their work. The children scuttled hither and thither, disappearing beneath the enormous looms. My heart raced as I thought of the danger that these poor children were subjected to in their workplace.

Nobody stopped. 'The overseers used to make sure that they didn't stop,' Sam told me.

The heat was almost unbearable and the noise was deafening. It would have been impossible to hear anything, but the people were communicating in spite of the noise. They did this by speaking in a strange silent exaggerated mode. 'It's mee-mawing,' chuckled Sam. Mee-mawing! I'd never heard of it! Apparently it is an old Lancashire term for talking to somebody in an extremely noisy environment without being vocal.

The scene faded and I was back in the present day. As I related what I had seen to the producer, a man in the world of spirit slowly started to build up quite close to me. He did not look English; in fact he appeared to be of either Italian or Spanish origin, with his dark hair and swarthy complexion.

'My name is Eduardo Silvano,' he said in heavily accented English. 'I worked here in this place for many years.'

As I reported this, Chris gasped and took a few paces closer to me.

The spirit of Eduardo Silvano continued, 'It was very hard work – punishing! The children! Oh the children! How they suffered, working from morning to night. They were sometimes so tired that they would fall asleep. That's when the accidents happened. I was an overseer here. I tried to be kind, but the owners wanted their profits. If I had been more lenient I would have lost my own job. That would have meant that my family would have starved. I could not allow that.'

While I was communicating with Eduardo I could see out of the corner of my eye that Chris was becoming more and more excited. When I finished speaking he could contain himself no longer. 'That's my grandfather!' he exclaimed. 'He worked here as an overseer and his name was Eduardo Silvano! How amazing!'

After a lunch break the camera crew and I walked around the outside of the mill, accompanied by Chris, who was still shaking his head in amazement that his grandfather had come through from the spirit world to tell us of the hardships of the mill in the days when the cotton industry was one of the major employers in the region. Being somewhat of an expert on the area, he was more than happy to confirm that the information I had been given by spirit was correct.

When the investigation came to a close I felt a little chastened to think of the comparatively easy life that we lead in these modern times with our children safely in schools and not having to literally risk life and limb for a few coppers to help the family finances.

The Hall i' th' Wood

Following the investigation of the mill, my next investigation was at the Hall i' th' Wood in Bolton, once the home of Samuel Crompton, who invented the spinning mule in 1779. This machine revolutionized the spinning industry and I was fascinated to see a full-size working replica standing in the main hall of this lovely old fifteenth-century house.

The Hall i' th' Wood was first opened as a museum in 1902. It had been the home of wealthy merchants for almost 400 years and was consequently steeped in the residual energies of the people who lived there. It seems impossible to believe that such a beautiful building would be let out as tenements, but this was the case in the eighteenth century, though the whole house was rented by the Crompton family from 1758 to 1785.

Because of the rich and varied history of the Hall, the emanations I received from the residual energy when entering the house were manyfold. As I walked from room to room I could pick up the energies of past residents through the ages, but it was when I reached the upstairs landing that I came face to face with my first spirit presence in the house. He was tall and wore a dark suit. His receding hair curled over the collar of a white shirt. This was Samuel Crompton. He was not a happy-looking man – more a man laden with troubles. Sam whispered to me that Samuel was not happy at all. He had made a number of business blunders over his remarkable invention.

I wandered from room to room, speaking as I did so of the energies I was picking up. There was a young lady, beautifully dressed and with long golden ringlets, who flitted from bedroom to bedroom, laughing as she went.

In the dining room I was impressed by the name 'Alexander' and a feeling of pride overcame me as I surveyed the length of what had once been an elegant parlour.

In the kitchen, which at the time I visited was being used as the museum office, I could see clairvoyantly the busyness of a working kitchen with maids running hither and thither. A little old lady in spirit sat on a chair near to the fire. I had the impression that she felt at home in the kitchen area, though I did not feel that she had the robust attitude of a cook. She certainly seemed to be very much at ease as she nodded and smiled at me.

All in all, the Hall i' th' Wood is a fascinating place to visit. I would certainly recommend it as a location for a paranormal investigation, providing of course that the correct permission is sought. I thought it a coincidence to visit a mill one week and the very next week to go to the place where the spinning mule was invented.

CHAPTER 9

Ghosts who Share our Homes

It may be easy to summon up impressions of ghostly monks and cavaliers within the walls of an ancient building. But it has to be remembered it is not only old buildings – castles, manor houses and the like – that are haunted. Longfellow's famous quotation 'Every house wherein man have lived and died are haunted houses' is stunningly accurate in that everywhere we go, we leave our residual energies and the more emotional those energies are, the stronger the impression they leave.

I have lived in various properties over the years. Most of my homes have had no resident ghosts but have merely been visited by the spirits of my family members, Sam and occasionally the previous occupants, who no doubt just called in to see what was going on in their old homes.

However, there was one large Victorian house in Liverpool where I lived for a while after my marriage to Joan had broken down which was occupied on a more or less permanent basis by two sisters who had passed to the spirit world but had decided they were going nowhere. They were staying put!

I moved into the house on a dark wet November day. Although the house was over 100 years old, it had been modernized and was bright and airy. I knew more or less immediately, however, that the past was still around. There would be a brief glimpse of movement on the stairs or I would catch sight of the whisk of a skirt disappearing around a corner or through a door. There was even one point in a wall in the hallway where I would see the figure of a woman seeming to melt into the wall. Upon investigating the area I found that what appeared to be a solid wall was in fact a sheet of plasterboard which had obviously been used to block up a pre-existing doorway. The plasterboard had been decorated to match the remaining hallway wall and I would have been unaware of the fact that a doorway had ever existed had I not seen the spirit lady appear to walk through it.

This is typical of the instances when people have reported seeing ghosts 'walking through walls'. Spirit people who choose to visit their old residences do not see them as they are now, but rather as they were in the days when they lived in the physical world. So they will continue to use the doorways they remember, even if the doors are now blocked up. Similarly, if a floor has been lowered they will continue to walk at the level of the floor when they lived in the house, thus giving the appearance of floating along above the ground. A ceiling may have been made higher, with the rather disconcerting result of people seeing ankles and feet walking across the top of the room. It is in fact the result of changing the level of the floor in the room above. In one or two of the properties I have investigated over the years staircases have been removed or relocated and people have reported seeing 'ghosts floating down from the ceiling'. The spirit people are not floating – they are using the staircase which they remembered from the days when they lived in the property in their physical form.

Within a few days of moving into my new home I had established that there were in fact two ladies in spirit occupying it with me. I had been feeling quite low for a day or two and on the third day I woke up feeling quite ghastly and with a raging temperature. I had 'flu. As I lay in bed, drenched in sweat and feeling far too ill to even attempt to get up, I saw the figure of a lady in spirit approaching my bed. She was quite small and rotund. She wore a longish dress of a smoky blue colour and had a pinafore tied around her waist. Her hair was grey and fashioned into a bun at the nape of her neck. Her face was round and rosy-cheeked and she had a kindly expression.

As she drew nearer to the side of the bed she reached out towards me and I felt a cool sensation on my forehead. Then I fell asleep. I slept for hours, waking briefly now and again, only to feel once more the cooling sensation on my face.

I awoke the following day feeling very much better. My temperature had dropped and I was able to make my way weakly downstairs to the kitchen to make myself a cup of tea. I still felt quite ill, but I knew that I was on the mend, thanks to the help of the spirit lady in keeping my temperature down. Nobody knew that

I was ill, as I had been too unwell to leave the house and at that time I could not afford a telephone. My only companion during that awful day and night had been the kindly soul who had eased my raging temperature.

I climbed back up the stairs and shakily changed the sheets that were damp with my sweat. I lay in bed once more and reflected upon my experience with the lady in spirit. Although I was feeling very much better now, I was still groggy and weak. I fell asleep once more.

I awoke in the twilight of the winter's afternoon. As I opened my eyes I saw that the spirit lady had returned. She was standing with her hands clasped in front of her pinafore, smiling at me from the corner of the room.

'Thank you,' I whispered.

She nodded her head to me.

'Who are you?' I asked.

'I'm Eleanor,' she told me. 'I live here with my sister Margaret and my brother Bill. My father had this house built and we lived here as children.'

She went on to tell me that she had married, but her brother and her sister had remained at home with their parents until they had passed to spirit, leaving Margaret and Bill to continue living in the house. When Eleanor lost her husband Ted to spirit she had returned to her childhood home and lived with her brother and sister. 'Ted and I weren't blessed with children,' she explained.

I continued to see Eleanor frequently around the house but I rarely saw her sister. Margaret was not a bit like Eleanor. She was tall and thin and always wore dark grey clothes. She never smiled when I saw her – in fact I had the distinct impression that she was not too keen on men at all and considered that I was trespassing by living in what had once been her family home. Eleanor would always look cheerfully at me and occasionally she would communicate with me, but Margaret never did. Of the four bedrooms on the first floor I always felt uncomfortable when walking into one of them. I assumed that this had been the bedroom occupied by Margaret when she had lived in the house in her earthly state.

I saw Bill once in the room I used as a dining room. When I walked into it one evening the scene that greeted me was nothing resembling my home. There was an old-fashioned fireplace with a number of easy chairs in front of it. In one of them sat a man. He had his legs stretched out in front of him and his head lay against the back of the chair. His hands were resting on the arms. To all appearances he looked as though he was asleep. It was very peaceful and quiet. I blinked a couple of times and the scene disappeared. I was left staring at my modern dining suite and a small table on which stood a pot plant.

I had noticed that an old man lived in the house next door and I thought he might remember the family, so one day when we both happened to be arriving home at the same time I asked him whether he recalled the people who had lived next door to him.

'Oh yes,' he said, 'I remember them well. I believe that they had lived in the house from the date it was built. The parents passed away, leaving the son and a daughter. The elder daughter had got married, but she moved back in when she lost her husband. The son Bill died about 20 years ago, but the two sisters, Margaret and Eleanor, lived there until they could no longer cope. Then they moved into a nursing home. They were old, though, and I heard that they passed away within a few months of each another.'

I remained in the house for another year or two. I was glad to share it with the family, even though I felt that Margaret was less than happy with what she considered to be my intrusion.

I have lived in two or three houses since then but the only spirit visitors I have had have been my own or Gwen's family members and of course Sam – until, that is, we moved into our present home.

The house we live in is less than three years old. It was occupied briefly by the family who built it on what had once been a market garden. Although the house is almost new, I am often aware of the movement of spirit people. They are the spirits of people who lived in the old house which once stood on the ground upon which our house now stands. They will not of course be aware of the modern building, but will be visiting the home of their memories.

I had just arrived home after a hard day's work when my telephone rang. Gwen asked me to answer it as she was in the middle of putting food out for our cats. I picked up the telephone and heard a voice telling me that it was Sophie Jennings and that she hoped I did not mind her calling me, though I did not know her. I asked how she had obtained my telephone number and she told me that a friend of hers had given it to her. She apologized for contacting me but told me that she was desperate to speak to me.

Sophie told me that she had recently moved to Churchtown, an area near to Southport. At first everything had been fine – she and her husband Rick had been overjoyed with their new house. Rick had recently left the army after serving nine years and had started a new job as a supervising security officer in Southport. He had decided that he would like to carry out some home improvements. Their new home had an unusual underground basement and he thought that he could convert this space into a leisure room and a spare bedroom. He decided that he would knock down two facing walls. When he did so he was surprised to find that behind one of the walls was what appeared to be a smaller room containing some bits and pieces.

'It all started from there, Derek,' Sophie went on. 'One night we went to bed and turned out the lights and for some reason I started to feel very cold, even though I was lying next to Rick and covered with a thick duvet. Rick asked me what was wrong as I lay there shivering. Before I could reply, he bolted out of the bed. "God Almighty! What was that?" he shouted. I hadn't seen anything. Rick told me that he had seen a large red globe-like sphere above his head and it had shot across the room towards the window.'

Sophie explained to me that Rick was a man who did not believe in the supernatural, a real sceptic. But then they had both heard a horrible sound, just like somebody hissing. They turned on the lights and went downstairs, feeling very scared and uncomfortable. They couldn't find anything amiss, but decided to stay up anyway and spent the night in the living room.

The following day they both went out to work but they hadn't forgotten the previous night's events and were still discussing them over their evening meal. After that, they began watching television, but the whole sequence of events started all over again just as it had the night before in the bedroom. This time Rick experienced the freezing cold sensation as well as Sophie.

For the next two weeks, both of them heard screeching noises every night in the cellar area where Rick had been carrying out the renovation work. He had been so scared that he had not returned to the basement to continue the job.

Finally, both of them were at their wits' end. 'I know, we'll call in a priest,' Rick suggested, 'or one of those people who talk to the dead! Medium, medium isn't it?'

I knew that I had to help this couple. I asked Sophie whether she would like me to come to their home to see what I could do. She readily agreed.

The next evening I arrived outside a pleasant-looking semi-detached house in Churchtown. I knocked on the door, which was opened by a woman in her mid-thirties who introduced herself as Sophie. She led me down a hallway and into the lounge, where Rick was waiting for us. I could see that both he and Sophie were very disturbed about the events that had been taking place in their home.

After a brief chat, I opened myself up to the vibrations of the house in general. I knew that I should not concentrate on the bedrooms but on the scene of Rick's renovation work. That was where the root of the problems lay.

As we descended the steps to the basement area, I could feel negative energy building up. I stepped down into the room and was immediately aware of an unbelievably horrible stench beginning to permeate the air. I staggered as I felt a blow across my shoulders. Sophie, who was standing on the bottom stair with Rick, screamed with fright. She then turned and retreated back up the stairs. Rick and I were left in the room on our own. 'Stay with me, Rick,' I said. 'Sam and I will sort this out!'

I quickly asked Sam what sort of entity we were dealing with. He told me that when Rick had started the renovation work he had disturbed the spirit of a man who was very agitated. As Sam spoke to me, the form of the man slowly built up before my eyes. He was of stocky build, but only about 5'6" in height. He was wearing dark-rimmed glasses and was going bald. He looked as though he was aged somewhere in his fifties. I had the distinct impression that he came from a era not too long ago, around the time of the Second World War. I attempted to converse with him, but he did not want to talk to me. Sam confirmed that this was the spirit man who had been causing all the problems in the house.

I turned to Rick and told him that I thought it would be a good idea if he joined Sophie upstairs, as I would like to try something that did not need his presence. Rick turned in a rather relieved manner and raced back up the stairs.

I asked Sam whether he could convince the man in spirit to converse with me so that we could help him. After a few moments I spoke to him directly. 'Can you speak to me?' I asked quietly.

'What d'you want?' asked the spirit man harshly.

'Who are you? What are you doing here?' I asked him.

'So many questions! Why are you in my house?'

The spirit man's reply showed me that he had not realized that he had passed over to spirit.

'What's your name?' I asked him.

'Ernie,' came the reply.

I asked him a few more questions, but I am afraid that he was less than forthcoming in his responses. I quickly gained the impression that he had been a very stubborn man in life, as he was definitely being extremely stubborn now!

'Is it wartime?' I asked him.

'You stupid, stupid man! Of course it is. Can't you hear the bombs?' he replied. Then he continued, 'I'm fed up with all this. Where's Millie? I can't find her anywhere. She's in trouble when I see her.'

I asked who Millie was.

'Oh shut up, man! She's my wife! Everyone knows that.'

I asked Ernie what he had been doing before seeing Rick and me. After a thoughtful pause he told me that he had had a fever and that Millie had gone out to get medicine for him. Whilst he awaited her return he had been lying on the bed they had made up in the cellar of the house. He and Millie spent quite a lot of time down there because of the bombs. Although Southport was not affected overmuch by bombing during the Second World War, obviously this pair had been very cautious and had preferred to spend their days in the safety of the cellar rather than make use of the rest of their home. Ernie said he had felt a pain in his chest and then everything had gone dark.

I sighed. I knew that I had to explain to him that he was no longer part of this physical life. He had obviously suffered a heart attack and passed to spirit on the day that Millie had gone out to buy medicine for him.

I did my best, but Ernie looked at me with a disbelieving stare. 'So you're telling me I'm dead! How can I be? You can see me, I can see you! You can hear me and I can hear you!'

I explained to Ernie that I was a trained medium and that mediums can see and hear people from the world of spirit. It took some more persuasion, but finally he relented and agreed that he might well have passed over. That would explain why these strange people had invaded his home!

'And they're not the first, you know!' he told me, glowering. He had also been wondering why all his belongings had disappeared. In the end he had decided to hide himself away in the basement in the small room that only he knew about.

'I wondered how I got in there, because there's no door,' he mused. 'I just thought myself in, and there I was!'

At this moment I heard a sound behind me. I turned and saw the lovely light spirit form of a lady.

She stretched her hand out to Ernie. 'Come with me, Ernie,' she said quietly. 'Millie's waiting for you.'

I watched as Ernie and the spirit lady slowly dissolved in to the atmosphere. No longer would Ernie endlessly search his old home for his wife. I knew that Sophie and Rick would be able to enjoy their home in future without Ernie disturbing them with his negative energy.

I trudged back up the stairs where Sophie and Rick were waiting for me. 'It's done!' I told them. I explained to them about poor old Ernie and his confusion. They seemed to feel sorry for the old man, but were glad that he had at last found peace on the heavenly side.

As they walked me to the front door Rick had one question for me. 'I was wondering, Derek,' he said. 'Who's Sam?'

CHAPTER 10

Incident at a Night Club

The last place you would imagine a ghost to appear would be a night club, but why not? If a person enjoyed the nightlife in their earthly existence, why shouldn't they enjoy the razzamatazz when they have passed on to the spirit world?

I recall being contacted by a local television company. The producer, Paul, had been told by the owner of a club on the outskirts of Liverpool that his staff were experiencing strange goings-on in the building. Paul asked whether I would be prepared to visit the club with him and see if I could tell them what was causing the problems.

I arrived at the club on the allotted day to meet Paul and his camera crew, together with John, the owner of the club. I asked John what had been going on. 'Lots of things really,' he said, 'but mainly glasses being moved and chairs being overturned whilst the club is shut for the night.'

I walked into the building. During the day a night club is not the glamorous place it turns in to once the sun has set and the street lights are on. The building I entered was brightly lit, illuminating the sparsity of furniture and the cigarette burns on the carpet. 'Dim lighting hides a multitude of things,' I thought to myself as I walked into the centre of the dance floor.

The cameras were rolling. There was silence. At night time music resounded off the walls of this huge building, but now it was quiet. The click of my heels echoed as I walked across the dance floor. I stopped at the side and listened. Sam was with me.

'What is the cause of all the activity' I asked him.

'Somebody wants to talk to you,' said Sam. 'Have a little patience, Derek!'

I stood quietly for a few moments longer. Then I became aware of a spirit person. He was a young man. He looked to me to be around 21 or 22 years of age. He had very short dark hair, was quite tall and slim and wore a striped shirt hanging outside his trousers. He was a good-looking lad. He had his eyes closed and seemed to be clicking his fingers to the rhythm of some music which was inaudible to me. As he materialized completely in front of me he opened his eyes and looked at me, giving a shy smile.

'What's your name?' I asked.

'Daniel,' he told me. 'I passed into the spirit world a year ago just outside.' He pointed to the door.

Daniel said that he used to visit the night club every Friday and Saturday. He lived with his mother, father and sister in one of the roads nearby. He used to love his visits to the club. He would meet all his friends there to relax for the weekend, dancing and enjoying the music. 'It was the gear!' he said. 'We had some great laughs.'

He went on to tell me that on a Saturday night about 12 months previously he had visited the club and, unusually, had had a couple more drinks than he was used to. He had decided that he would go home early as he wasn't feeling too well. He had slipped out on his own without telling his friends, as he didn't want to spoil their fun. To reach his home he had to cross a busy main road. Because he wasn't concentrating, he had begun to walk across the road without looking out for oncoming traffic and had been hit by a car. His spirit had left his body instantly.

As Daniel was talking I related all the information to Paul and John. 'I remember that incident,' John said to me. 'It was really sad because that lad and his friends never caused me any trouble, but why's he doing what he's doing, and why is he here and not with his family?'

Daniel smiled. 'I like it here,' he said. 'If I try to move anything at home Mum and Dad always say it's Tracey, my sister, not putting things away properly. The only way I can get a message to Mum and Dad to tell them that I'm OK is by doing things here. I know that John is always on the lookout for a bit of publicity, so I thought that if I moved stuff around here he'd get in touch with the papers or the telly, and they'd bring a medium in. Mum wouldn't think of going to a medium herself, because she's a bit afraid, and Dad thinks it's all a load of hocus pocus.'

I smiled as I relayed the information. It wasn't the first time I'd heard about a dad who used that phrase.

Daniel told me that his mum or somebody who knew her would see the item on the television and that he wanted me to say that he was OK, that his mum and dad weren't to worry about him. He wasn't in that cold hole in the ground – he was here, enjoying himself and listening to his friends just as he always had.

As I was telling Paul what Daniel was saying, I heard John shout to me, 'Well, I can't see anything. You just look as though you're standing there talking to yourself! If Daniel's there, ask him to do something – to move something maybe.' He smiled as he said this, and nudged Paul in the ribs.

Daniel looked at me and chuckled. 'Some people won't believe at all, will they, Derek? Watch this!'

Just as he finished speaking we all heard a creak high up in the ceiling about 15 feet above us, where the lights were suspended from a gantry. We all looked up. As we did so, a lens from one of the lights came crashing down onto the floor.

Paul rushed over to pick it up. 'It's impossible for this lens to come loose on its own!' he said in amazement.

'Well, John did ask!' said Daniel, laughing.

John was looking very much less amused now; in fact he looked quite pale – far from the giggling sceptic of a few minutes earlier.

'Would you do something for me, Derek?' Daniel asked. 'Would you make sure that you say in the interview that I'm OK so that Mum and Dad know that they should stop worrying about me. I'm well and with Nan. She's been taking care of me.'

'Of course I will, Daniel,' I told him. He smiled as he slowly faded from my view.

I walked over to Paul and John and the other people who were present. 'That was amazing,' said John. 'You've certainly changed my mind, Derek.'

I told him that I hadn't done anything, that it had been Daniel. 'You asked and he responded. You should get some good publicity out of this!' I laughed.

John looked sheepish and I knew that Daniel had been correct.

The following day the item was aired on local television. Afterwards the company was contacted by Daniel's family, who requested a meeting with me. I was more than delighted to agree and was able to tell them that Daniel was happy, well and still enjoying nights out with his friends.

CHAPTER 11

A Call to the Local Radio Station

I recall being contacted by a DJ named Peter from a local radio station. A lady called Sandra had written to him from her home in the Wirral to tell him that she was being bothered by strange occurrences in her kitchen. Lights would be switched on and off randomly, the kitchen was always cold, no matter what steps she took to heat it, and she was also aware of a feeling of being watched when she was in the room. She was very worried and asked whether Peter could help her by contacting somebody who might be able to assist her with this strange and alarming situation.

I arranged to meet Peter at her house later that week. We arrived at the appointed time outside a modern semi-detached house no more than ten years old and were met at the door by Sandra. She ushered us into a bright sitting room where she told us of the curious events she had been experiencing.

I asked Sandra to take me through to the kitchen area. Immediately I entered I felt the atmosphere change. I doubt whether this could have been picked up by any equipment, but it would easily have been discernible to a sensitive such as myself. However the sudden and dramatic drop in temperature would easily have been registered by the most rudimentary of thermometers and would have been noticeable to anyone walking into the room.

I looked around. There were all the usual items of kitchen equipment – a cooker, toaster, kettle, washing machine, etc. My attention was drawn to the refrigerator, which was standing in a small alcove close to the back door.

'You've had problems with the fridge/freezer,' I stated.

'Yes,' Sandra agreed. 'There have been countless problems and yet the engineer can find nothing wrong with the thing.'

'I think you'll find that your problems are being caused by a man in spirit who has links not with this house, but with a building which previously stood on this land,' I told Sandra. She agreed that before the small housing estate in which she lived had been built, a farmhouse and outbuildings had stood on more or less the precise location of her home. I described the man to her and although she told me that she had never met the farmer, she was well aware that he had been a bad-tempered loner who welcomed nobody onto his land. I told Sandra that after he had passed to spirit, he very much resented the fact that a distant family member had sold the farmhouse and the land to a property developer. He was demonstrating his displeasure by coming into her house and causing the problems she was experiencing.

'I know you have two children,' I said. 'Would one of them be a very sensitive boy?'

She agreed that her son Adam was indeed a most sensitive and shy child.

'The spirit man is using Adam's energies to help him in his destructive ways,' I told her. 'The way to go about this is for me to close Adam's psychic energies down to the man and from there on in, he will be unable to get up to his tricks, as he won't be strong enough.'

Sandra was a little dubious, as she thought that her son might have to take part in some form of ritual, but I assured her that all I would need to do was to meet Adam and hold his hand for a moment or two. More than a little relieved, Sandra agreed that I should call again when Adam and his sister Stephanie were there. I warned her that it would be best to empty the fridge/freezer and turn it off until I returned, as I felt that the spirit man, knowing that I was about to cut off his lifeline of energy, would attempt to cause quite a big problem with the piece of equipment as a last act of defiance.

Sandra said that she would do as I suggested, but I knew that she would not. I was not surprised, therefore, to receive a telephone call from her the following day to tell me that the fridge/freezer had blown up and a fire had narrowly been avoided. I made an arrangement to call later that day to meet Adam after he had finished school.

I am happy to report that after meeting Adam and his sister I was able to put an end to the problems that Sandra and her family were experiencing due to the old farmer who so resented the happiness of this young family on the site of his old home.

I am of course often contacted by people requesting my assistance with 'hauntings' in their homes. Unfortunately not all of these requests are genuine.

I recall another occasion when I was contacted by a radio station. I was asked to accompany their representative, Robert, to the house of a lady who insisted that she was being bothered by all manner of disruption for which she could find no cause. Again, it was a relatively modern house, but I could feel nothing in any part of it which would suggest the presence of a disruptive spirit.

The lady of the house showed me a room where she told me that clothing had been thrown around. According to her, the clothes had been neatly put away in a wardrobe. I was shown upturned plant pots and even stains on the ceilings and walls.

I was perplexed, as I could sense nothing untoward in a spiritual sense. I looked closely at the stains on the wall and asked for a damp cloth. Sure enough, when I rubbed the marks, they disappeared. Then I heard a whisper from Sam. At his suggestion I looked over to the door, which was ajar. I saw the mischievous face of a boy in his early teens peering in. I knew immediately that he was the author of all the disruption. The poor lady had been tricked by her young son into believing that there was a 'ghost' in her house when in fact it was merely a practical joke that had gone too far.

I gently told the lady that there was nothing of a paranormal nature going on in her home and that she would have to look to a more worldly cause, nodding towards the giggles which were now clearly audible behind the door. The lady was aghast. She had truly believed that a spirit person was causing the chaos in her home and she was embarrassed that she had brought me out on the basis of a schoolboy's prank. I assured her that she should not worry; that I was happy to know that she now had peace of mind and knew that there was no demonic spirit lurking in her cupboards.

CHAPTER 12

Animal Ghosts

Many are the reports of spectral animals stalking the fields and lanes. The countryside teems with headless horses, ghostly dogs and the wraiths of long-gone cats. The majority of my experiences with animals, however, have been far more heart-warming.

I have conducted many personal readings for people when, to their surprise, I have described a cat or a dog which has come to them during the course of their reading. On many occasions the people have been surprised and said to me, 'Oh! That's our old pet Bobby [or whatever their pet's name happened to be]. I didn't think they went anywhere when they died!' Of course they do! Animals pass on to the spirit world in exactly the same way as we do. They are creatures of God. Why should they be any different from us?

Gwen and I have a great love of animals and have experienced the anguish of losing a beloved pet to the world of spirit on a number of occasions. I have written in *The Psychic Adventures of Derek Acorah* of the passing to spirit of Cara, my German Shepherd dog, at the grand old age of almost 17 years. We were fortunate and privileged to have her share part of our pathway in this life with us. What was harder to bear was the passing to spirit of our beautiful Bonnie at only seven years of age in the spring of 2004, and even more recently, in December 2004, the going over to spirit of one of our cats, Jasper, again at only seven years old.

It is at times like this that the old question 'Why?' is raised. The answer is that it was meant to be. Just as we have life's experiences to encounter, so do animals. Bonnie and Jasper came into this world with their life's pattern before them, just as we do. Our life's pathway is preordained before we incarnate into this earthly life.

Of course, as with most people, there have been a couple of 'happy endings' concerning our pets. The first I recall was a cat which belonged to Gwen when she and I first met many years ago. His name was Boo and he was a ginger tom of some considerable vigour and standing in the local feline community. Gwen moved house, taking Boo with her, and he gradually established himself in his new area and seemed to settle into his new home. His favourite place was the top of the wall at the bottom of the garden, where he would sun himself throughout the day.

One evening Boo did not come home. He had disappeared without trace. Day after day Gwen and I searched and searched, calling his name, all to no avail. The days turned into weeks and the weeks turned into months, but I knew that Boo would return home.

'How can you tell me that, Derek?' Gwen would say with some frustration.

I knew that Gwen was passionate about her pets and I was not offering her false hope – that would have been too cruel – but I knew that Boo would one day return to live with Gwen once more.

A year went by. Gwen spoke of Boo less and less, but whenever the subject did come up I knew that she did not believe me when I persisted in telling her that he would come home.

'Sam's told me,' I would say.

'Well, tell Sam he's wrong!' Gwen would reply with some asperity.

The weeks continued to pass. One day I was sitting in my office in Liverpool when the telephone rang. It was Gwen. She told me that she had been looking through a bedroom window which overlooked the back gardens of the houses beyond. On the lawn of the house directly behind hers she had seen a ginger tomcat who looked very familiar, but because ginger toms are not such a rarity she thought that maybe her neighbour had acquired a cat of that colouring.

'Go and ask,' I suggested to her. 'Remember that Boo has a nick in his ear which will identify him to you.'

That evening when her neighbours returned home Gwen knocked on the door and asked about the ginger tomcat in their garden.

'He's a stray that I've been feeding,' the lady said. 'He's been coming here for a few days now, but he's not here at the moment.'

Gwen explained about Boo and asked her neighbour if she would be kind enough to telephone her the next time the ginger cat appeared so that she could see whether it was in fact her missing pet.

A couple of days later the neighbour telephoned to say that she had the cat in her house. Arming herself with a cat basket, Gwen went along to see him. A little later I received a joyous call to say that Boo had come home! He had recognized Gwen and gone to her straight away.

We can only speculate as to what had happened. What we do know, following a veterinary examination and X-ray, is that Boo had a couple of shotgun pellets lying close to his spine. He had obviously been shot at by some evil person, run off and got lost. After hiding away somewhere to recover from his injuries he had eventually wandered back to his old stamping ground, but had been unable to exactly locate his old home.

Since then Gwen has never doubted my reply when one of our cats has been a little late in coming home. 'Is he alright?' she will ask. Fortunately I have always been able to reply, 'Yes, he is!'

This was never more amply demonstrated than in 2003, when our cat Toby disappeared without trace.

Days went by with the inevitable 'Is he OK, d'you think?' from Gwen.

'He's fine,' I would tell her. 'He's got himself stuck somewhere – he can't get out, but he's not starving or distressed.' I could see Toby enclosed in some way. I also knew that a woman would be instrumental in getting him home, though as he is a rescued feral cat and will not let anybody but Gwen near him, I did not quite know how this would be brought about.

As usual when one of our cats disappears for more than a few hours, the RSPCA was informed and our neighbours were treated to a leafleting campaign asking them to look in their sheds, garages or outhouses for a black and white cat. This time there was no response whatsoever and as three or four weeks went by I was beginning to see that Gwen's faith in my prediction was beginning to waver. 'Don't worry,' I would tell her. 'He'll come home. Remember Boo?'

A few days later I received a telephone call from a lady who lived in a farm across the fields from our house. She told me that she had been away from home and had arrived back to find our leaflet. She had gone to check that there were no cats locked in any of her outhouses and when she opened the door to an empty stable, a black and white cat had shot out and run off into the fields in the direction of our house. She asked me whether our missing cat had returned home. At that point I had to tell her that he had not.

I told Gwen, who immediately ran down our garden, scrambled through the hedge into the fields which separate the lady's farm from our home and started calling Toby's name.

Suddenly, through the long grass of the field, she saw a black tail heading in her direction. It was Toby!

He had come home! We were both so delighted and relieved. Even the other cats seemed pleased to see him.

Toby has never strayed far since. He seems to have learned that he is safe in his own garden.

Unfortunately, not everybody experiences happy results such as these. There have been occasions when beloved animals have gone missing and the owners have consulted me and I have had to tell them that their pets have passed to the world of spirit, but that they will meet up with them once more when they themselves pass into the world beyond.

They may see them before then, of course. It only follows that just as we can choose, after passing to spirit, to revisit the homes we have lived in, so animals can return to the places where they have been loved. This explains the reason why there are so many reports of houses being 'haunted' by dogs, cats or other animals. They are merely returning to visit their old habitats.

I have often seen Cara, and more lately Bonnie, in our new home. They are happy and together. They come to visit us to let us know that they are aware that we have moved home but that they still love us and look forward to us all being together again. No doubt they call in to their old home as well to wander around the garden they enjoyed so much in earthly life. I look forward to the time when Jasper returns to let me know that he is with his favourite friend Bonnie, whom he loved so much when they were here with us.

Our friend Patricia Smith wrote the following poem for Gwen and me after we lost Bonnie. I hope that anybody who has also lost a pet will read these beautiful words and take comfort. I hope that they will also realize that to take on another dog or dogs is not being disloyal to the pet you have lost – they understand that there arc those among us who just do not feel complete without a furry friend at our feet.

The Paw on the Stair

*They say you'll always return
And visit your favourite place
Where love was all you knew,
And to gaze on your favourite face.*

*We found it hard to say goodbye
But we really do believe
That we needed to be together
Though we'll never truly leave.*

*We're running through the fields now
So happy to be alive
We know you're sad without us
But our spirit will survive.*

Please be happy with the new ones,
Who have come to take our place.
We know they'll bring you joy and
* love*
And fill up that empty space.

Our lives with you were perfect
And the love was forever there
So always believe we're with you
When you hear the paw on the stair.

Patricia Smith (2004)

CHAPTER 13

Theatre Ghosts

I am fascinated by theatres and find them to be very satisfying locations to investigate. There is nothing like the atmosphere of a theatre – the excitement of the cast, the expectations of the audience, the dramas of the productions. All these emotions are retained in the fabric of the buildings. When everybody has packed up and gone home and the auditorium is quiet and deserted, the memories remain. The theatres then become the domains of the ghosts of people who trod their boards and who lived out their dreams and their dramas within their four walls.

I do not think that there are many theatres in England that do not have a ghost or a haunting. During my theatre tours around the country I am frequently told, 'We have a ghost, you know. Have you seen it?'

Liverpool Theatres

My home city of Liverpool has a number of theatres, all of which abound with stories of paranormal sightings.

In the Liverpool Empire there have been numerous sightings of a young girl who fell to her death from the circle into the stalls. It was unfortunate that I was unable to join the International Society for Paranormal Research on their investigation of the theatre, as described in my book *The Psychic Adventures of Derek Acorah*. I would have welcomed the opportunity to join the team as they walked through the rabbit warren of corridors and stairways. However, the spectral presence I would really like to have investigated is the 'black phantom' who once dwelt in Dressing Room S. It used to be said that when the dressing-room door was opened, a black shape would be reflected in the mirror opposite. Performers would refuse to use the room because it was always cold and dark. Since the theatre was refurbished in 1998 the black phantom has apparently disappeared, but I wonder…!

Other theatres in Liverpool also have their resident ghosts. The Royal Court Theatre plays host to Les, once a handyman there, who was clearing out the grids when he slipped and broke his leg. Unable to get back into the building, he passed away due to exposure, as it was icy weather at the time.

A woman named Elizabeth is said to haunt the gallery of the Playhouse Theatre. She worked as a cleaner in the days when it was a music hall and variety theatre. She fell into the orchestra pit after being hit by a fire iron whilst cleaning the stage.

Also at the Playhouse, a grey lady has been seen in the corridor outside the upstairs rehearsal room and the ghost of an elegantly dressed upper-class woman is said to roam from the coffee bar to the stalls. A spirit man in Edwardian clothing has been also seen in the stalls coffee bar area, pacing up and down as he searches for his daughter, who ran away to join a theatre company in the early 1900s.

Lastly, the Everyman Theatre men's toilets are regularly visited by a man in spirit who switches on the hand dryers, even though the electricity supply has been turned off. Staff often report seeing a dark shadow and hearing ghostly footsteps at the back of the auditorium as they lock up for the night.

The Edinburgh Festival Theatre

Even though I was unable to investigate the Liverpool Empire, I have been given the opportunity to explore many other theatres. One investigation that stands out in my memory was at the Edinburgh Festival Theatre.

I had been asked by Granada to conduct an investigation for the television programme *Predictions with Derek Acorah*. We arrived at the theatre just after lunch on a cold March day. The wind was biting, so we were more than pleased to be shown into an empty dressing room, which was to be our base during the investigation and filming.

After a warming cup of coffee I was taken through to the auditorium. Nothing could have prepared me for the magnificence that greeted my eyes. I had thought that this was a modern theatre, as we had entered through a huge glass-fronted structure. Now I could see the full grandeur of the theatre's heritage.

I stepped onto the stage and opened myself up to the vibrations of performances over the years. I was surprised at the impressions I was receiving. I was being shown scenes of old music-hall performances such as I had seen as a child on the television programme *The Good Old Days*. I was made aware of animals on stage – performing horses and dogs – and a myriad of acts – acrobats, comedians, jugglers and magicians. Names I recognized from the old black and white movies I had watched in my youth rang in my ears – Marie Lloyd, Charles Laughton, Laurel and Hardy and Charlie Chaplin. I could hear the big-band music of Joe Loss in the background. It was a fascinating experience.

I left the stage and followed the crew through the meandering corridors backstage. As I did so I glimpsed the silent wraiths of yesteryear. A man in spirit appeared. He had obviously been a stagehand. He was dressed in working clothes of the late Victorian era. He was proudly going about his business. As he did so, he saluted my presence by touching his cap and murmuring, 'Good evening, sir!' before hurrying away in the direction of the stage. I decided that I would retrace my footsteps and follow him.

I reached stage left and stood in the wings for a moment. As I looked towards the stage, a scene built up before me. Centre stage stood a man. He was dressed in a long black cape which appeared to cover evening dress. He had very dark collar-length hair and sported a dark goatee beard and moustache. He was walking from the back of the stage area towards the front. He had obviously finished his performance and was about to take his final bow.

'This is the Great Lafayette,' Sam whispered to me. 'He was a great illusionist in his day. Everybody came to see him.'

The Great Lafayette appeared oblivious to my presence as I walked onto the side of the stage. I hoped that I would be able to communicate with him.

As I stood gazing out over the vast auditorium which rang with the sound of long-gone applause, I began to smell smoke. I heard the crackling of flames on the stage behind me. I turned but there was nothing – only the camera and sound crew recording what I had to say about the scene I was clairvoyantly viewing.

'What happened, Sam?' I asked my spirit guide, fearing that I had witnessed a disaster of mammoth proportions. I knew that an audience of well over 2,000 people must have been in the theatre at the time.

'This was the great illusionist's final performance,' Sam told me. 'He lost his life that night, together with some backstage staff. The audience escaped.'

As I looked out over the auditorium once more I heard one of the crew shout out, 'What's that, Derek?' He pointed towards the rear of the theatre. 'I'm sure I saw something move!'

I looked towards the area where he was pointing. Sure enough, there stood the Great Lafayette dressed in his long black cape. He stood still for a moment and then slowly dissolved and disappeared from view.

The theatre staff member who accompanied us on our walk around the theatre confirmed that what I had said was correct. In 1911 the Great Lafayette, together with 11 other people, had succumbed to the effects of a fire at what was then known as the Empire Palace Theatre. This had been caused by a stage lamp falling and igniting scenery during one of the illusionist's performances. The audience had escaped, as the safety curtain had been immediately lowered, minimizing the spread of the fire. The Great Lafayette had been buried in Edinburgh alongside his beloved dog Beauty, who had passed to spirit just days before the tragedy at the theatre.

CHAPTER 14

Ghosts of Long Ago

The most obvious place to conduct a ghost hunt is in an ancient building. Care has to be taken, however, that the correct permissions are obtained and it must always be remembered that you are a visitor to somebody else's property.

Here are a few of the investigations I have undertaken at old buildings and my encounters with the ghosts of long ago.

Vale Royal Abbey

Vale Royal Abbey, deep in the Cheshire countryside, is now a golf club. It had been chosen as the location for an investigation that would form part of the programme *Predictions with Derek Acorah*. I had some difficulty in finding the place, so was grateful for directions from a local policeman.

As I drove through the gates and along the drive I could see the abbey in the distance. Although there were a few golfers with their trolleys going to and from the building, the air of ancient tranquillity remained.

I was met at the door by Sophie, my producer. She introduced me to Norman, who was the caretaker and historian for the day.

I felt steeped in the peacefulness of monastic life as I walked from room to room in the old abbey. Time after time I caught fleeting glimpses of monks as they went about their daily life in service to God and his people. In the library the temperature was so low that I shivered, even though it was a warm summer's day, and I caught a glimpse of a woman in a nun's habit standing staring out of the window.

We went through to the Great Hall. 'There has definitely been spirit activity here,' I stated. 'I feel that people have noticed the movement of cutlery.'

Norman agreed that this had indeed happened and said that people always felt as though they were being watched in that room.

I knew that these ancient walls contained a secret. 'What's the secret?' I asked Sam. 'What is it that makes me feel this air of something unusual?'

Sam chuckled. 'That, Derek, is because amongst all the monks who lived and worked here, there was a nun – Sister Ida!'

A nun! In a monastery! I had never heard of such a thing. I turned to Norman and told him that Sam was telling me that a nun had lived here amongst the monks.

A strange expression flitted across Norman's face. 'I know!' he said. 'I wondered whether you'd be able to tell me that.'

I had the strangest feeling that Norman was a little in love with the memory of the holy sister of long ago. I was hesitant to tell him what Sam was telling me: 'Sister Ida fell in love with Abbot Peter. He saved her – he gave her refuge at the abbey.'

Ida had apparently taken refuge in a nunnery after being promised in marriage to a man she did not love. She had been befriended by one of the fathers at the abbey, Father John.

Norman nodded his head vigorously when I passed on the information Sam had given me. 'Can you tell me anything more, Derek?' he asked. 'I feel that Ida is seen frequently by people who work here. She looks out from the window. She is very sad.'

Sam continued the tale. Father John had been made abbot and had taken the name of Peter. One day whilst travelling with one of his monks, he had been attacked. He had been brought back to the abbey, where Sister Ida had tended him until he had passed on to the spirit world. Sister Ida had loved her friend the abbot. Upon her own passing to spirit she had been buried alongside him.

Norman said that what Sam had told me was true. He was able to add that in 1740, whilst the cloister walls were being pulled down, two coffins had been discovered. They contained the bodies of an abbot and a nun.

We left the abbey and walked out onto the field which lies in front of it. Approximately 50 yards away I could see what appeared to be a stone water trough.

As I approached it I had the strangest feeling. I looked down into the water. To my horror I saw the body of a young woman. As I continued to stare down, her face became clearer. I could see that she had been very beautiful, with long flowing fair hair.

The vision in the water faded from view. I turned to Norman and told him what I had seen. I added that I had been impressed with the name 'Meg' and with the knowledge that she had lived in a village nearby. I was perplexed by the mention of a village, as we were surrounded by fields and the only building in sight was the imposing old abbey.

Norman nodded and smiled. 'That's a stone coffin, Derek,' he said, nodding towards what I had thought was a water trough. 'Can you tell me any more about the village?'

'I don't know,' I replied. 'I'll try!'

I gazed across the field and felt an urgent need to continue walking towards the far side. We were almost three-quarters of the way across it when I stopped. I could hear something. It sounded like hoofbeats on hard-packed earth. I looked around the lush green field, then closed my eyes. When I opened them once more the field had disappeared. In its place I could see a small group of houses. There were people, too, dressed in clothes made from rough-looking cloth, a type of woven wool. There were no bright colours, just dull browns and greys and the occasional glimpse of a woman's pale-coloured head-cloth. The people appeared to be going about their daily lives. It was in fact the scene from a hamlet of many years ago.

I heard a clashing noise behind me and turned around. Two men were fighting. They were large men and wore what looked to me to be thick leather breast-plates. Their forearms were bare, but I could see that they were slightly better dressed than the crowd which had gathered around them. They were wielding large swords. As they fought one another their lips were drawn back from their teeth with the effort of battle and their long hair flailed around as they moved. Suddenly one man stumbled and went down on one knee. His opponent grasped the opportunity to bring his sword down with a sickening blow to the side of his head. As quickly as the image had appeared, it was gone.

Once more I turned to Norman and told him what I had seen. 'There was a small village here,' he told me, pointing to the very ground we were standing on. 'We have come across many artefacts to support that. In fact there are still some stones around which formed part of the houses which stood on this very spot!'

I looked towards a small copse of trees at the edge of the field. 'And there's the burial ground!' I murmured.

'D'you think so, Derek?' said Norman. 'We've been searching for that for a long while but so far have found no trace.'

We retraced our steps across the field and returned to the abbey. I reached my car and shook hands with Norman as I bid him goodbye. As I drove away I could see him waving and hoped that I had not disillusioned him too much and that he would continue to revere Sister Ida as much as he ever had.

Smithills Hall

My first visit to this manor house situated on the outskirts of Bolton was again during my days with Granada Breeze. Smithills Hall, with its creaking staircases and small latticed windows, is everybody's idea of a haunted house. It is easy for the visitor to imagine the ghosts of yesteryear drifting through its corridors. For the intrepid ghost hunter, however, Smithills Hall is rich in history. I defy anyone to investigate this location and not experience some kind of paranormal phenomenon.

My second visit to Smithills was in the company of that intrepid ghost hunter Avid Merrion in the guise of 'Craig David' for his cult programme *Bo Selecta*. Prior to the airing of the programme I was criticized rather severely in some quarters for taking part. It was said that as a spiritual medium I was bringing Spiritualism into disrepute. I thought that was rubbish! Being a Spiritualist does not mean that your sense of humour disappears. A medium is an ordinary person with an extraordinary gift – the gift of communicating with the world beyond. However, when people finally viewed the segment of the programme in which I appeared, I think that they were pleasantly surprised at the sensitivity with which the *Bo Selecta* team had treated my work.

My investigation took place on a day in April 2004. I travelled to Smithills Hall in the early evening, managing to get lost on a couple of occasions *en route*. I eventually arrived around 6.30 p.m. and was introduced to a quiet auburn-haired young man in the kitchen surrounded by the debris of a very late lunch. I had expected Avid Merrion to be the totally extrovert person who appears as his various alter egos in *Bo Selecta*, but no, he was quiet, unassuming and polite. I was to meet the 'public' Avid Merrion a little later.

Smithills Hall is the home of one of the strangest anniversary hauntings, that of the famous 'bleeding' footprint which is sited in the passageway just along from the chapel. It is said to belong to George Marsh, who was convicted of heresy and sentenced to burn to death in Chester. As he was led from the court, which had been held in an upper room of Smithills Hall, he is alleged to have raced down the stairs and stamped his foot upon the stone floor, shouting as he did so, 'If I am true to my faith, God shall leave his mark!' It is at this very spot at the foot of the staircase that a clearly discernible imprint of a man's foot can be seen. This imprint is said to turn wet and red every 24 April, the anniversary of the burning of the martyr George Marsh.

As I waited for Avid to don his chosen outfit, I opened myself up to the emanations and vibrations of the old hall. It was growing dark and the house was settling creakily for the night. The quiet of the kitchen was disturbed by the sound of footsteps. The door opened and I was greeted by the vision of a man in a khaki boiler suit. There was a strange can-like contraption strapped to his back. A piece of vacuum-cleaner hose with some sort of nozzle attached to it was looped over one arm and on the other was balanced the most unrealistic rubber kestrel I have ever seen. A catheter bag half full of a yellowish liquid dangled from one side of his webbing belt. This was balanced on the other side by a toilet roll suspended on a piece of string. The man's face was disguised by a large rubber mask and topped with a woolly hat. A pair of spectacles which magnified mild blue eyes three-fold completed the ensemble.

'Right, Derek! We're ready to go,' said Avid's voice from the mouth gap in the mask.

I doubled up with laughter. How on earth was I going to conduct an investigation in the company of this 'vision'?

We proceeded outside so that 'Craig David' could introduce the segment of the show in which I was to appear. The quiet Avid Merrion was no longer there. In his place was the extrovert and talented man who attracts audiences of millions. In his own inimitable way he introduced his viewers to Smithills Hall, explaining to them that he was joining Derek Acorah of *Most Haunted* in an attempt to discover whether there were ghosts at the old Lancashire hall.

On entering the hall I knew that we would not be disappointed. The air hung heavy with the memories of events that had taken place within these ancient walls. The producer took me on a short walk round the ground floor so that I could adjust to the atmosphere. I was aware almost immediately that there was a spirit person following us.

'Are you picking anything up, Derek?' the producer asked.

'Yes,' I replied, 'but I'd sooner not talk about it until we start filming.'

We returned to the rest of the crew, who had completed filming the introduction with Craig David. Now it was my turn to be questioned. The words 'Craaaaaig David seeks it out!' rang out in the old building. Avid's eyes flashed maniacally as he turned to me saying, 'Now, Derek Acorah! What does it feel like to see and talk to ghosts?'

I replied that these days, after so many years, my work was becoming more normal and natural to people.

'Take this down!' yelled Craig David. 'Normal and natural!!! That's *normal* and *natural*!' He jabbed his finger downwards. 'And are there any ghosts here today?' he continued.

I said that indeed there were. I told him of the spirit presence I had noticed whilst I was walking around with the producer.

Craig's eyes flicked from side to side. 'All this talk of ghosts is upsetting Kes,' he said indicating the plastic bird on his arm. At this, it started spinning round. I could hardly speak for laughing. I wondered desperately whether I would be able to continue with the investigation.

We began walking slowly along a passageway. Suddenly I became aware once more of the man in spirit who had followed me earlier. I stopped.

'What's wrong, Derek?' asked Craig nervously.

I told him that there was a man with us who was not too happy that we were there. 'He's telling me that his name is Richard and that he would like us to leave his home.'

Craig looked even more nervous. I gained the impression that the spirit man was a little annoyed because he thought that we were being disrespectful.

'Don't worry, Derek,' Sam said. 'I will explain to Richard that no harm or disrespect is meant.'

I turned around to look at Craig. As I did so, I saw a lady in spirit suddenly appear directly behind him.

'D'you feel anything behind you?' I asked.

Craig leapt forward, uttering a few expletives. 'Can they touch you, Derek?' he asked shakily.

'Of course they can,' I told him.

'It's alright for *you*,' he replied. 'You do this every day of your life!'

He looked so nervous and his reactions to what I was saying were so funny that once again I dissolved into laughter, but we had to continue with our investigation.

I took a few moments to compose myself then apologized to the lady in spirit, who had remained in the atmosphere. She kindly informed me that she was a 'Barton'. I took her to be the lady of the house. I felt that she had resided there physically some time around the sixteenth century.

We went upstairs and entered a large room that had very old polished floorboards which were creaky and uneven.

'Oh no!' I said as I viewed the scene that was unfolding before my eyes.

Craig David leaped forward, turning around as he did so and pointing his 'ghostbusting gun' in the direction I was looking. 'What can you see?' he asked. 'I don't like it in here.'

A very loud bang could be heard. It came from the far corner of the room. I could see a number of spirit people in the room. One man was deeply distressed. He was being verbally and physically abused by a group of men who were around him. It seemed to me to be some type of court-room procedure. The words 'Renounce your church, heretic!' rang out to my clairaudient ear. This must have been the trial of George Marsh, who suffered for his faith and finished his days so horrifically in Chester.

I could see a spirit man sitting at a long desk. Sam told me that this was Roger, the magistrate, conducting his court.

I related all that I was seeing to Craig David, who appeared to be growing more and more nervous by the minute. 'Where do all these people come from?' he asked me.

I told him that most of what I had experienced had been energy which still remained in the fabric of the building, but that both the spirit lady and Roger did come back to visit quite often.

We went back downstairs to the front door. Craig said, 'What an experience, Derek. We certainly had some paranormal activity here tonight. We all felt something going on. I can't explain it, but this is what it's like when you're in the company of Derek Acorah.'

Pompeii

I have been fortunate in that I have been given the opportunity to visit very many interesting places during my years as a medium. One such place was the ancient city of Pompeii.

Situated near the Gulf of Naples, Pompeii was devastated by the eruption of Mount Vesuvius in AD 79. A large number of people lost their lives due not only to inhaling poisonous gases but also to the tidal wave that hit the Gulf of Naples after the eruption. Volcanic ash and showers of small stones then buried the city and all its occupants. It was not until the sixteenth century, whilst excavation work was being undertaken in order to dig out a canal, that the ruins of Pompeii were discovered.

I was fascinated upon my arrival at Pompeii to see how perfectly preserved the city was. Although the roofs of the buildings had collapsed under the weight of the fallout, the architecture and many details of the homes and municipal buildings still remained.

As I wandered through the ancient city streets, I could sense the residual energy of the busy day-to-day life that had taken place almost 2,000 years ago. I walked from the Forum, the main square, stopping to look at the temples of Apollo and Jupiter. Then I wandered along Via Della Fortuna. As I did so, I came upon a fountain in the middle of the dusty road. It was an elaborate fountain with a large central piece surrounded by a stone basin. At the edge of the basin was an indentation from people who had leaned their arms there as they had stretched forward to take a drink. I was curious to see whether I would pick anything up if I rested my hand on this spot. As I placed my hand in the indentation, I felt a surge of spiritual energy go up my arms to my shoulders and then on up to my head. I had taken on the energy of a spirit person who seemed to be smaller than me in height but much broader in the shoulders and body. My arm seemed to become very muscular and strong. I looked down to my wrist. Gone was the modern watch that I was wearing. In its place was a golden amulet inscribed with letters that I could not decipher. I began to experience a feeling of agitation. Clairvoyantly I viewed a scene where I was walking at a fast pace to a home which was beautiful both inside and out. I shook my head and brought myself back to the present, although I felt a definite urge to find the house I had been shown.

I walked rapidly down a road between the remains of houses and shops. Through alleyways I went, along roads I did not know, until I looked up and saw the magnificent front of what appeared to be a dwelling. There were two enormous columns on either side of what remained of the doorway. I walked through and into an area of floor tiling the like of which I had never seen before. Strangely, though, I felt at home. I knew that somehow, in some way, the spirit person whose energies I had experienced had been connected to this building.

I carried on walking through the gardens of the house. I noticed the statue of a woman, quite small in height, standing in the corner of the garden. When I touched it I had the impression that this statue was connected to the man whose spirit I had so recently experienced and that they had been members of an important family in the days when Pompeii had been a thriving city.

The impressions faded and I retraced my steps to the street in front of the house. I felt reluctant to leave the peace and tranquillity of the beautiful garden, but knew that I must not allow the spirit of the man who had influenced me to remain with me.

I continued to wander down Via Stabiana and turned left into Via Dell'Abbondanza. Everywhere I looked there were the remnants of the life of the old city. There were the suburban baths, a theatre, a house of ill repute, a bakery complete with oven, and houses with wonderful wall paintings.

On I trudged. The heat was becoming unbearable. I reached an area where I could look down onto a smooth grassed square surrounded by tall columns on three sides and a long shed on the fourth side. I felt a tingling and a rush and once more I was being taken back to the times when Pompeii was at its greatest. As I looked at the square of grass I could see men, heavily muscled and tanned, wrestling with one another and throwing each other to the ground. It was obvious to me that there was no animosity involved in their battles, that they were merely sportsmen practising for the main events. I realized I had reached the gladiator barracks. This was where the men practised their sports and honed their dexterity with spears and lances before travelling across the city to the amphitheatre where up to 20,000 people would watch the bloody shows performed by the gladiators and wild animals.

My time in Pompeii was over. It was time to travel back to Naples to my hotel. But I vowed to myself that one day I would return to Pompeii to continue my investigations into the lives of the people who once lived there.

CHAPTER 15

Ghosts Abroad

Wherever we go, we will always be in the company of the spirit people who were there before us. Whether we are in a modern-day metropolis or a tiny African village, the spirit world will be there too!

Anne Frank's House

Whilst travelling around the world I have visited many places, each with its own atmosphere and spirit presences. But none has ever touched me as much as my visit to the house in Amsterdam where Anne Frank and her family lived for two years in hiding from the German forces during the Second World War.

Anne Frank was born in Frankfurt in 1929. By 1942 life for Jewish people in Germany had become restricted. To avoid deportation to the so-called 'work camps', Jewish families had to arrange a hiding-place. Otto and Edith Frank arranged to go into hiding in an annexe of the building where Otto conducted his business. They were to be joined by friends of the family, Mr and Mrs Van Daan, together with their son Peter. A little later a dentist named Mr Dussel would join them. In all, eight people were to share the cramped living quarters for a little more than two years before their secret annexe was raided by security services. They were all arrested and transported to concentration camps. Only Otto Frank survived.

I was surprised when I arrived at what is termed 'Anne Frank's house' in Amsterdam. Here was a modern building containing bookstalls and various large screens showing photographs of Anne Frank and displaying her original diaries in glass cases. My companion nudged me. 'Don't be silly, Derek. You'll see in a moment!'

Sure enough, a few minutes later I was being led towards a bookcase which swung aside to reveal a narrow staircase. As I clambered up the stairs to the cramped living quarters I was overwhelmed by the rush of mixed residual energies. There were feelings of fear, love, compassion, hatred and what I can only describe as a deep and abiding dread – the dread of being discovered must have hung heavy in the hearts of all occupants of these rooms.

From room to room we went. There was no spirit activity – I did not expect to see any. I doubt very much whether spirit return would ever take place here, though the residual energy retained was some of the strongest I have ever experienced. Maybe it was because there were so many people cramped into such a small place; maybe it was because emotions would have been running high over a protracted period of time. What I do know is that I was touched by Anne Frank's hiding-place more than any other location I have ever been to.

They came on trains
some barely alive
The young and the old
trying hard to survive.

Above the gates
'Work Makes You Free.'
These would be the last words
many would see.

They hoped for liberation
at the end of the track,
They hoped for freedom.
Millions never came back.

Evil was waiting
a conveyor belt to hell.
Their lives became torture.
They died where they fell.

Young and old taken
through the gates en masse,
not knowing they were going
to the chamber, to the gas.

How power can corrupt
and lead to hell on earth
when a living, breathing person
has no worth.

Lessons must be learnt
and people must ask why
or but for the grace of God,
there go you and I.

Patricia Smith (2005)

Westminster Hotel

A number of towns and cities that I have visited retain the memories of the First and Second World Wars within the fabric of their buildings.

I recall visiting the Westminster Hotel in Le Touquet, northern France. It had been taken over by the German forces during the Second World War and used as their headquarters. The residual energy still remains and the spirit of a high-ranking German soldier wandered through my bedroom as I prepared myself for a night's sleep.

The Spirit of Ned Kelly

During my footballing days in Australia I visited many places where the spirits of days gone by still walked, carrying on as though they had never departed from this physical life.

I had felt drawn to the Australian Aborigine culture and had become a friend of Vladimir Botesni, who was the curator of the Adelaide Museum. Vlad and I some-times talked about famous and sometimes infamous Australians, one of whom was Ned Kelly. Once, when I was due to travel from Adelaide to Perth, Vlad suggested that I might be interested in stopping at a small township close to Kalgoorlie where Ned Kelly was reputed to have stayed many times.

The following week I set off on the gruelling journey, which would take me over the Nullarbor Plain, a desert region in South Australia, and on to Perth – a total distance of 1,796 miles. I had planned on taking four or five days to do the drive, which would give me the opportunity of staying at the township suggested by Vlad.

It was an amazing journey along the straight bitumen roads flanked on either side by red sand and scrappy shrubs in temperatures of up to 43 degrees. It was strange not seeing anything for hundreds of miles, with the exception of the odd emu and a bird of prey devouring the carcase of a kangaroo which had fallen victim to one of the few cars travelling along the road.

After two days, it was with some excitement that I realized I was only about 100 miles from Kalgoorlie. 'I'll be there in an hour or two,' I thought to myself. I was keen for a shower and something to eat.

I carried on driving for a little longer, then I saw in the distance some wooden buildings which were surrounded by a wooden-railed fence. As I slowed my car I noticed that the front door was open and outside stood a sign telling everybody that 'Ned Kelly stayed here!' This was too good an opportunity to miss! In spite of my hunger, I decided to stop and take a look.

I was greeted by a very nice lady who told me she was the owner of what turned out to be a small guest-house. I asked whether she had any rooms available for the night, as I had decided to spend the rest of the day there rather than carry on to Kalgoorlie.

'I don't suppose the room where Ned Kelly stayed is available?' I asked.

'I always get asked that,' the lady laughed, 'and you're in luck! The room's vacant!'

She handed me the key and told me the times when food was available.

I was quite disappointed when I opened the door to Ned's bedroom. I had expected something a little larger than the tiny room which contained a single divan bed and miniscule wardrobe. On the wall by the bed there was a tiny mirror and there was a small window over-looking the back of the house. Nevertheless I was glad to unpack and to bathe in the small bathroom. What a relief it was to feel clean.

After about an hour I left the room and ventured through to a lounge housing a display of paraphernalia and merchandise connected to Ned Kelly. Then I wandered outside, where signs led me to a museum.

As I went in, the first thing that I saw was what appeared to be a very rough suit of armour. This was what Vlad had told me about in our conversation back in Adelaide. The armour bore no resemblance to the medieval suits of armour we often see in the UK – this was merely rough-hewn metal sheets joined together with what looked to me to be like links of a chain. The helmet was round but straight-sided and had a flat top. There was an opening at the front through which the wearer could see. The card next to the armour bore the words 'Ned Kelly's plate armour'. Apparently the famous criminal had worn this whilst carrying out his notorious raids.

I was asked whether I would like to try and put the suit on. It looked very heavy and cumbersome, but I was willing to give it a try. It was useless! It was just so heavy. I don't know how on earth a normal man could lift, never mind wear, the thick steel plate armour. The lady in charge of the museum told me that Ned Kelly had been known for his massive strength and had been able to lift great weights over very long periods of time. I was shown some old photographs of Ned and some other criminals who were well known in the area in those times.

I wandered back to the main building and returned to my room. As I put the key in the door I heard a loud bang from inside the room. I walked in and looked around, but there was nobody there and nothing had been disturbed. I began to take a few items of clothing from my bag. As I was doing so I became aware of a spirit presence moving around the bedroom. I said quietly into the atmosphere, 'Who are you? Show yourself if you can.'

Minutes passed by, but the spirit person was not willing to let me know their identity. The temperature in the room had dropped dramatically. When I had entered, the atmosphere had been warm and stuffy, but now it was cool and rather chilly.

I began to feel rather uncomfortable. Suddenly one of the wardrobe doors swung open. There was a loud rap on the window.

'Whoever you are, are you displeased with me?' I asked into the ether.

With that, my bag, which was on the bed, suddenly overbalanced and dropped onto the floor.

'That's enough!' I said quietly. 'Whoever you are, you're going to have to put up with me for this evening.'

The proprietress of the guesthouse called me to my evening meal. After we had eaten I sat and chatted with her for quite a while. She told me what she knew about Ned and his life. It was a fascinating conversation. At around 10.30 I decided that I would retire to my room, as I wanted to make an early start and carry on to Perth.

As soon as I entered my room once more, I was aware that a spirit person was there.

'Show yourself,' I demanded. 'Is it you, Ned Kelly?'

A smell began to pervade the room. It was a horrible smell – that of an unwashed human body. Gradually it disappeared, as did the spirit person. I went to bed and fell asleep almost immediately.

I was woken at around five o'clock in the morning by noises which seemed to be coming from the head-board of the bed. I looked up and saw the face of a spirit man. His eyes were menacing and dark. His hair looked dirty and unwashed. The face disappeared. I then saw a shadowy figure move across the room at great speed, though it disappeared before I was able to discern who or what it was.

Everything fell quiet and I dropped off to sleep once more. I woke at seven and got out of bed. As I turned to look out of the window something caught my eye. There, tucked in the edge of the mirror by the bed, were two photographs of Ned Kelly and his accomplices. I know that nobody had entered the room during the night because I had locked the door and the key was still in the lock. Had anybody attempted entering with another key, my original key would have been pushed from the keyhole and would be on the floor. Although I had opened the window in an attempt to allow in some cool night air, the whole window area was covered with a close mesh metal netting that had been screwed to the frame of the window. I was at a loss as to how the photographs could have got where they were.

I went through to breakfast. As I did so I was stopped by the proprietress, who asked me whether I had had a good night's sleep. I told her what had happened and handed her the photographs I had found tucked into the mirror frame.

She did not seem in the least surprised. 'That's Ned!' she laughed. 'He's always doing things to try and frighten people. He doesn't like people staying in his room in case they find out any of his secrets! Did I tell you the room was haunted?'

CHAPTER 16

The Most Haunted

I have often been asked where is the most haunted location I have ever investigated. I imagine that people expect me to name a famously haunted castle, manor house or inn. In truth, the most haunted place I have ever visited is a rambling old farmhouse on the outskirts of Merseyside. Unfortunately it is a private home and I am therefore unable to identify it.

I was asked by the owners, George and Sue, to visit their home with a view to discovering just what was going on there. As they explained it, 'We feel as though we're living in the middle of Oxford Circus, there's so much going on!'

I was intrigued. People had complained to me about all sorts of activity in their homes – items being moved, fleeting glimpses of something out of the corner of their eye, or even poltergeistal activity, but never had I heard anybody tell me that they felt as though they were outnumbered in their own home.

As I arrived at the farmhouse, I was astounded that such a lovely home could be so close to the centre of Liverpool. 'If only the film and documentary makers could show this as part of northern life,' I thought to myself. 'They only ever show cobbled streets and back-to-back houses!'

I drove on to the farmyard, which was surrounded on three sides by outbuildings. The fourth side of the yard led on to a grassed area, beyond which lay what appeared to be a huge orchard.

As I sat in my car admiring the whitewashed house, I saw a movement on the other side of the yard. It was a man in spirit dressed in what I can only describe as typical farm worker's clothing. He had some leather harnesses over his arm and carried a huge collar of the type I had seen used on carthorses during my childhood. I watched, fascinated, as he disappeared into one of the outbuildings.

I began to understand what George and Sue had described as I alighted from my car. I felt as though I was in the middle of a busy farmyard, with people moving hither and thither, though apart from the spirit man I had just seen I could see no one, clairvoyantly or otherwise.

I walked over to the farmhouse door and knocked. George opened it. 'I was just coming out to find you, Derek,' he said. 'We heard your car pull up, but then nothing happened. We were wondering where you'd got to.'

I explained about seeing the man in spirit and the feelings I had experienced getting out of my car.

'Oh, we've seen that chap lots of times,' George told me. 'We call him Fred. He's around so often, I almost feel that I should be paying him wages! This place was a shire horse stud about 100 years ago, so we think that he may have been a worker here in those days.'

George led me into his home. Sue greeted me in the enormous living room. It was typical of an old farmhouse, with large dark beams and many doors leading from it. The atmosphere did not feel uncomfortable – in fact it was quite welcoming – but I was immediately aware that there was a huge amount of spirit activity within the walls. The whole place seemed electric and 'busy', as though I had stepped into a house where lots of people were living and lots of children were running around. It was almost as though they were in the next room.

Sue led me into the kitchen, where we sat and had a cup of tea while George related the history of the house as he knew it. He told me that the original farm was listed in the Domesday Book, which meant that there had been some sort of building on the land for 1,000 years or more. He knew that it had originally been a single-storey farm building, but approximately 500 years ago a second storey had been added, together with a new wing. It had been used by nuns as an orphanage for a number of years, but had then reverted to being a farmhouse. George knew it had been a shire horse stud in the early twentieth century because he had been visited once or twice by a very elderly man who used to work there as a groom. Then it had been used as a small dairy farm up until the early 1960s, when George had purchased it

'Don't get me wrong, Derek,' he said. 'We love the place and we wouldn't move. We're not bothered at all by our "visitors", because we feel at peace with them, but after seeing you on the television we thought you might be interested in coming and having a look for yourself.'

George and Sue took me around their home and I began to see exactly what they meant when they said they lived in a busy household. There were many spirit people, all from different eras, going about their daily lives. I caught a glimpse of housemaids going about their tasks, there was a bustling cook in the kitchen and there was the residual energy of children's laughter and the serenity of holy sisters as they whisked around taking care of their charges. In the upper levels it was the same – odd glimpses of people from yesteryear, all behaving exactly as they had done in their physical life.

There was only one room in the old house where I picked up anything other than warmth and good feelings. As I entered a bedroom I immediately felt I was being watched by somebody or something that really did not welcome my presence – or, for that matter, the presence of any other person. There were feelings of resentment in the atmosphere.

I opened myself up to the vibrations of the room. 'Who is this person, Sam?' I asked.

'Edward,' Sam told me. 'This is Edward.'

He proceeded to tell me that Edward had been the second son of the owners of the farm and had unfortunately been a disappointment to his father. Not being quite as bright as his older brother, he had been treated quite abominably and had been dismissed as being 'stupid'. He had been a quiet child and as he matured his resentment towards his father had grown and he had developed into a morose man who shunned people, preferring to spend his time on his own in this bedroom.

As I related my findings to George and Sue, they nodded in agreement. 'That would be old Edward Armitage, poor old chap,' said George. 'He was a bit slow and his father was ashamed of him, always favoured the older son Sid. The previous owner told us about him – he was still living here with his mother when we bought the place. The father had died and the older son had gone off to Australia or somewhere. Apparently Sid wasn't interested in farming – he felt he was much too clever! I heard that Edward passed away a couple of years after leaving this place. He couldn't get over having to leave.'

I explained to George and Sue that the reason for the high incidence of spirit activity in their home was the age of the building. It had also obviously been a happy place, in whatever capacity, and so the people in spirit felt that they wanted to return to it. The only exception was poor old Edward. There was also an enormous amount of residual energy, which contributed to the feeling of activity all the time.

'But I feel that there's a mystery you haven't told me about,' I told George.

He laughed and told me that I was correct.

'Would I be right in saying that this mystery doesn't involve the house but is set in an outbuilding?' I asked.

'Correct again, Derek!' he said. 'But can you tell me any more?'

I asked to be taken into the yard. As I stood there concentrating, I felt that I was being drawn to a shed which was attached to the huge barn which ran along one side of the farmyard. 'It's in there,' I stated. 'That's where the mystery lies!'

We walked over and entered the shed. 'There's water – a well,' I said, 'and that's where the mystery is. The answer to the question being asked is "no".'

I looked at George to see whether he could make any sense of what I was saying. 'Well, that's a bit of a disappointment,' he told me. 'We'd heard that there was a secret tunnel leading from this well to an abbey some four miles away. We thought that it added a bit of a mystery to the old place, but obviously the story's incorrect.'

I was sorry to leave George and Sue's home. It was a lovely place – an oasis of peace and calm, but not too far away from a busy city. The atmosphere was also welcoming and happy – not at all how you would imagine a 'most haunted' house!

CHAPTER 17

Your Stories

Each week I receive numerous letters from people who write to tell me of their own experiences with the paranormal. I thought that I would share a few of these stories with you.

Dick Turpin?

I received a letter from a Nikki who once lived in Kenilworth Gardens, Shooters Hill, London. She told me that she had experienced some very odd goings-on in and around her baby son's bedroom. The room was always extremely cold. One morning she found the mobile above her son's cot was totally knotted. Her baby could not have done this, as he could not even lift his head. A few nights later, Nikki awoke to find the words 'Help me' written in the pile of the carpet outside her son's bedroom.

At that time, the family had an *au pair* living with them. The poor girl would be woken at three o'clock in the morning by the radio playing in the kitchen. She would have to get up, go downstairs and switch the radio off. The family began to suspect that there was an unexplained presence in the home.

One day Nikki came home and asked the *au pair* whether her husband was at home. The girl replied that though she had not seen him, she had heard him walking around in the house. When Nikki went to investigate, her husband was nowhere to be found, though the door to her son's bedroom was firmly shut – something which nobody made a practice of doing.

Thoroughly frightened by the events taking place in the house, Nikki called in the local vicar, who told her that he had received many similar reports from residents in the neighbourhood. He stated that Dick Turpin had operated widely in the area and he was inclined to think that he was the spirit presence responsible for the ghostly activity in his parish.

A Dark Presence

Diane and her family have lived in the same house for 26 years. As far back as the family can remember there has always been paranormal activity there.

One night Diane's mother had a rather disturbing experience. She went to bed and though she was still awake, she found that she could neither move nor open her eyes. She could not breathe and felt as though there was a tremendous weight on her chest.

On the same night, Diane's sister went into their mother's bedroom and noticed a dark shadowy figure sitting on the side of the bed. She tried to wake her mother, but was unable to do so.

For the following few nights the mother had exactly the same experience. At their wits' end, the family called in a medium, who conducted a cleansing ritual. That night when Diane's mother went to bed, instead of the usual crushing and paralysing sensation she now experienced a bright white light. Through this light she could see a corridor in her home with the figure of a man running away from her. He seemed frightened, as though he was running away from something.

From that day to this, Diane's mother has never had a recurrence of her terrible experiences. The family know, however, that there is still a spirit presence around. The television often changes channels of its own accord, the scent of flowers can sometimes be smelled around the home and there have been many more small signs. The family knows, though, that the only people in spirit who share their home with them now are the loved ones who have passed to spirit before them. They are no longer bothered by the dark presence that made their lives so miserable.

'Have We a Ghost?'

Dave is a family man, with a wife named Sue and two sons, Daniel and Paul. One evening, on going to bed, he popped his head into his sons' bedrooms to make sure that all was well. They were tucked up in bed asleep. Leaving their bedroom doors ajar, Dave went off to bed himself.

The following morning Sue told Dave that she had had a very strange experience. She had woken up at approximately three o'clock in the morning and had noticed a light coming from Daniel's bedroom. As she was about to get out of bed to investigate, the light appeared to turn from white to a deep electric blue and to ooze onto the landing area which lay between Daniel's bedroom and Dave and Sue's. At this point, it seemed to take the shape of a human form. Sue said that she hadn't felt afraid but in fact had experienced a sensation of calm and well-being.

For a few weeks nothing more happened, but after a while Sue experienced exactly the same thing again. A few days later, Dave woke up in the early hours of the morning to see the serene-looking spirit of an old gentleman smiling benignly down at him as he lay in his bed. It was time to find out what was happening!

Dave and Sue took themselves off to the local Spiritualist church, where they spoke to one of the mediums. 'Where do you live?' she asked. They told her, adding that they had bought the house about 12 months earlier. It had been the former home of a local doctor who had sadly passed over to the world of spirit.

'I know the place well,' the medium told them, 'and I knew Dr McDonald when he was still with us.' She added that she did not even have to visit their home to tell them exactly what was happening. What they were experiencing was the spirit return of the good doctor.

He was visiting his old home and walking around the rooms where he had lived for so many years. There was nothing to be afraid of, as he would not harm them. In fact the blue colour they were seeing was a sign of healing. If they were afraid, however, all they needed to do was ask the doctor to be a little more circumspect in his visits. He would understand.

Dave and Sue returned home a little bemused, though they thought that they might try doing as the medium had suggested the next time they had a night-time visitation.

A week or two later the doctor in spirit paid yet another visit to his old home and Dave and Sue asked him if he would please not make his presence quite so obvious, as they were afraid that their sons would wake and be frightened. As they made their request, the bright light faded. They have never seen it again. They do, however, notice that from time to time small items in the home are moved about. It is obviously the good doctor doing his rounds.

'We Are Not Alone!'

Jim wrote to tell me that he had lived in his house with his wife and three children for about six years. The house had a good atmosphere, but they had become aware of what they felt might be a spirit presence. To quote Jim: 'Every six months or so, basically just as you start to wonder whether you have dreamed everything, another minor thing will happen which confirms it all again in your mind.'

Jim stated that neither he nor his wife was particularly sensitive to the spirit world, but neither did they dismiss it. They did feel, however, that their home had a strange calming effect upon them.

Jim recalled arriving back home one dark night. As he got out of his car he began to feel scared and uncomfortable. The moment he reached his door and opened it, the feeling disappeared.

One of Jim's children had been unhappy going upstairs alone and had always insisted on taking his sister with him. At first Jim and his wife had thought that maybe their son was scared of the usual childish things such as monsters in the cupboard – that was, until the boy started to tell them about the old lady who came and sat on the end of his bed at night. He described her to his parents: she was small and slim with grey hair and always wore a cardigan 'just like Grandma Joan'. Grandma Joan was Jim's mother. She lived a mile or two away and was still well and truly in the physical world. Jim's wife's mother, however, had passed away a few years previously. She had been small and slim, had had grey hair – and had always worn a cardigan! Unfortunately she had passed over to the spirit world before her grandson was old enough to remember her.

Jim and his wife felt that in all probability the old lady who was sitting at the end of their son's bed was his grandmother. They did not want their son to be frightened, nor did they wish to offend the spirit of Jim's mother-in-law by telling her to stay away. Indeed, they welcomed her presence, as Jim's wife derived a great deal of comfort from knowing that her mother was still around them. They decided to follow the recommendations of a friend of the family who 'knew about spiritual stuff'. They asked the spirit woman to remain around them and share their home with them, but to take care not to frighten her grandson. At some time in the future he would be able to accept her visits, but at the present time he was a little too young to understand.

The 'spiritual stuff' obviously worked, as after that the young lad was able to go to bed without being disturbed by his doting grandmother. No doubt she still visits his bedroom and potters around in her usual way, but she no longer allows herself to be seen by her grandson.

A Sceptic!

Don wrote to tell me that for many years he had been a sceptic when it came to matters of the spirit world. He had been brought up a Catholic, but the whole idea of spirits being amongst us had never been of any importance to him.

Some years ago he had been house-sitting with his parents for an elderly aunt who had been in hospital at the time. Her house had been in the countryside and been part of a small community where everybody knew one another. The old lady had been married for over 40 years, but her husband had sadly predeceased her some 15 years earlier. Since then, whenever family members had visited the house, they had always noticed that the presence of the lady's husband hung strong in the atmosphere.

Don wrote that one day when he had been alone in his aunt's living room he had seen the spirit of his late uncle. He had not been frightened by the experience, rather felt a sense of great warmth, and he had known that his uncle was there to watch over the house.

The incident had passed from Don's mind after a while, then a young man he worked with had had a motoring accident and had unfortunately passed to spirit. Don had only met the man on a few occasions, but after the accident, whenever he had entered the office where the young man had worked, he had felt his presence as strongly as though he had been physically in the room. 'I felt as though I could almost reach out and touch him,' he wrote.

On another occasion, whilst sitting in the house of an acquaintance, he had been able to give the name of a man who had formerly been connected with the house. The owners had been astonished. 'The information just popped into my mind!' Don explained.

The final straw for this now wavering sceptic was during an evening out at a restaurant in an old building. As he had been sitting at the table with his friends, he had seen the hazy body shape of a woman float across the room. He had asked the people he was with whether they had seen anything, but no, they'd seen nothing at all! 'I think they suspected I'd had a little too much to drink,' wrote Don wryly.

CHAPTER 18

Where to Go

In my experience you can travel anywhere in the United Kingdom and not be disappointed in your search for haunted properties. There are cities which claim to be the most haunted in the country, and although some, such as York, Edinburgh and London, may produce more ghosts per square mile than other, wherever you live you will have many haunted locations to choose from.

Richard Felix, renowned ghost historian, would argue that the most haunted area of the country is his home town of Derby, 'the dead centre of England'! As this gentleman has dedicated 15 years to uncovering data to support this claim, who am I to argue with him? But I am sure that every ghost hunter, no matter where they live, will have no difficulty in finding somewhere worthy of their attention. There are castles and manor houses, mills and breweries, theatres, shops and hotels, as well as airfields and battlegrounds throughout the UK where there have been claims of ghost sightings.

Roman soldiers are said to silently march across our land, particularly in areas around Northumberland, where remnants of Hadrian's Wall are still to be found.

Ghostly battles still take place at Flodden and Bosworth and many other scenes of historic conflict. Our moors are said to abound with spectral creatures, although my only personal experience of this is limited to two sets of glowing ghostly eyes in the middle of Bodmin Moor. I was accompanied by Richard Felix at the time. After a frantic dash across the rain-sodden moorland to retrieve a torch from my car, I found the owners of the eyes were two wet and miserable-looking sheep!

Even our road system boasts a number of places where people have been convinced that they have run somebody down in their car, only to find that the 'person' has disappeared completely. Less commonly there have been reports of drivers being flagged down by a stranger to whom they have given a lift, only to find when speaking about the incident that their passenger has been a ghostly hitch-hiker.

There follows some suggestions as to where people who are interested in conducting an investigation may like to go. I must emphasize that I have not visited these places myself and so cannot guarantee that you will find a ghost. However, these locations have long had reputations for ghostly goings-on, so I am sure you will not be disappointed!

Pluckley

Two villages vie for the title 'Most Haunted Village in England'. These are Pluckley in Kent and Prestbury in

Gloucestershire. The 1998 edition of *The Guinness Book of Records* names Pluckley, but I doubt whether there is much to choose between the two of them.

Many of the reported hauntings in the village are connected to the Dering family, who arrived in Pluckley many centuries ago. They continued to reside in the area until World War I. It seems sensible therefore to start any investigation at St Nicholas's church, where many of the family are buried.

The church also boasts a number of hauntings. Mysterious lights are said to shine from the windows of the Dering chapel and ghostly knockings have been heard there. Lady Dering, who passed to spirit whilst still a young woman and who was considered a great beauty in her time, is said to walk the graveyard at night. Dressed in the exquisite gown in which her husband buried her and carrying a red rose, she drifts amongst the gravestones looking for who knows what. A lady dressed in a flowing red gown has also been seen in the graveyard. It is believed that she is yet another member of the Dering family, one who tragically lost her newborn baby. Her voice has been heard calling plaintively for her lost child. A large white apparition of indeterminate shape has also been seen floating across the gravestones, scaring more than one late-night reveller wending their way home. Inside the church the spirit of a small white dog has been witnessed running amongst the pews and a lady in modern clothing has also been seen, though her identity is unknown.

The Dering family occupied several houses in the village, all of which have been the scene of strange events. In one house, loud whispering is frequently heard. In another, an invisible entity tries to push people down the stairs. The bagpipes and the drums of the Highland Regiment have been heard by the occupant of yet another house. Dering Manor itself burned down in 1952, but a white lady is said to haunt the site. No doubt she is another member of the Dering family revisiting her old home.

At the Black Horse Inn furniture is said to move by itself and a phantom coach and horses has been seen.

Dicky Buss Lane is named after an unfortunate schoolteacher who is said to have hanged himself. His ghostly body has been seen swinging from the overhanging branch of a tree.

Park Woods is home to the ghost of a soldier who committed suicide by shooting himself. His wraith, known locally as 'the Colonel', has been seen walking through the woods on dark and windy nights.

The aptly named Fright Corner is the site where a highwayman was cornered by a group of redcoats and run through with a sword. He was left dying, pinioned by the sword to an oak tree, whose stump remains there to this day. The silent re-enactment of the scene is said to take place on bright moonlit nights.

An occupant of Elvey Farm has reported objects being moved and thrown across the room by some unseen force. The smell of burning has been noticed and ghostly footsteps have been heard pacing the floor.

The full moon sees the ghost of a miller at the old derelict mill. He wanders forever seeking a lost love.

By a small stone bridge at the crossroads the ghost of an old gypsy woman has been seen. It is said that she fell asleep whilst smoking her pipe and it fell from her mouth and set fire to her clothing. Her ghostly form has been seen huddled in a shawl.

The screams of a man who fell to his death in a clay pit terrify passers-by.

Numerous other reports of strange knockings and glimpses of people from the other world have been reported in many of the houses and cottages that make up the village of Pluckley.

Prestbury

Prestbury also has more than its fair share of ghosts. The High Street itself plays host to many of the phantoms of the village. There have been reports of a singing ghost in one of the cottages, an old lady who wears a large hat is regularly seen in the kitchen of another house and two of the shops report ghostly activity. A young lady in servant's garb has been seen floating across the road and a ghostly motorcyclist is reported to travel along the High Street before suddenly disappearing. A very inquisitive female entity goes from house to house looking in through windows, only to disappear into one of the eighteenth-century cottages. The ghostly form of a jockey in racing silks has been seen outside the King's Arms, but his identity is unknown.

Cleeve Hill sees the mournful sight of a phantom Victorian hearse and a spectral man walks the pathway leading down to the old racecourse.

Reports of ghostly monks abound both in the High Street and in Deep Street, whilst a further monk haunts the site where Morningside House once stood. There have also been reports of marching men, a small flock of sheep, horsemen and dispatch riders. Even a phantom tea party has been reported to take place in a field close to Prestbury House.

Perhaps the most famous of Prestbury's ghosts is the Black Abbot, who regularly walks from St Mary's church at Christmas, Easter and on All Saints' Day. Those who have seen him report him as quite solid and life-like. He has been seen on the road, in the church and in the churchyard, usually in the early morning.

All this, together with the sound of ghostly voices, inexplicable glowing lights and various 'grey ladies', makes Prestbury the equal of Pluckley when it comes to reports of paranormal events.

If you feel that you would like to visit either of these two villages, however, please do remember that many of the ghostly sightings have taken place in people's homes. There are many reputedly haunted sites in both villages that are available to the public, but respect must be shown to the residents of the villages at all times.

Littledean Hall

Chingle Hall near Preston in Lancashire has long been heralded as 'the most haunted house in England'. Although it boasts a number of spectral beings within its walls and gardens, I feel that Littledean Hall in the Forest of Dean, Gloucestershire, should be the true holder of the title.

The present Littledean Hall, built in medieval times, stands on the site of older footings dating back to Saxon times.

The best-known story of the Littledean ghosts dates back to 1741 when a young black servant murdered his master, Charles Pyrke. The servant and his sister had been brought to England as children from the West Indies by the Pyrke family. As they were of similar age, Charles Pyrke and his young servant had grown up together at the family home. In his early twenties Charles had raped his companion's sister and she had become pregnant. The family did away with the resulting child and hid its body behind the panelling of one of the bedrooms. Such was the anger of the girl's brother at this that he killed Charles. He himself was put to death as a result of his actions and his ghost, dressed in red robes and carrying a candle, is said to walk around the hallway and landings of the house.

Visitors walking up the staircase of Littledean often complain of feeling sick and dizzy. This is allegedly the influence of the spectre of an old stooped man who is thought to have fallen down the stairs after suffering an attack of vertigo.

There are several haunted bedrooms at Littledean. A blue lady gazes out of the window of one room; another lady, who is always reported to look sad, even though she is dressed in bright yellow, haunts a second bedroom; a third bedroom contains a shadowy figure who is reported to push the occupant out of the bed; and yet another bedroom is home to the ghost of a lady who holds a similarly spectral monkey.

The ghosts of two Pyrke brothers who shot each other dead whilst arguing over a young lady haunt the dining room, as does the spirit of a child. It is unknown whether this child is male or female due to the practice in former times of dressing little boys in similar clothing to that of girls. A monk in a white habit has also been seen in the dining room from time to time, but the noisiest ghostly inhabitants of this room are two duellists whose clashing swords have been heard. It is alleged that an indelible bloodstain remains on the floorboards, hidden beneath the carpet, marking the spot where the fatal thrust was delivered.

Strange smells and inexplicable noises have been reported throughout the house, particularly the scent of roses and the aroma of cooking in the kitchen area. Flower arrangements have been disturbed by some unseen hand.

The grounds also have their fair share of ghostly visitors. A hooded figure which floats along the driveway is thought to be that of a Roundhead captain during the English Civil War. A ghostly monk drifts around the gardens and spectral presences have been seen around the remains of a Roman temple in the grounds. It is alleged that animals were offered as sacrifices there to the goddess Sabrina, protector of the river Severn, as bones have been discovered in the area.

All in all, I consider that Littledean Hall richly deserves to be known as the most haunted house in England.

Speke Hall

It would be remiss of me not to make mention of one of my home city's most famous haunted houses, Speke Hall, built in 1490 by Sir William Norris.

Speke has a famous 'white lady', said to be the ghost of Mary Norris, who inherited the estate from her uncle, Richard Norris. The story goes that Mary was preyed upon by an inveterate gambler, Lord Sidney Beauclerk, who was rather unkindly known as 'Worthless Sidney'. They married and shortly after giving birth to their first child, Mary was told by her husband that they faced financial ruin because of his reckless gambling and would have to sell their home. As a result of this, whilst still in shock, she threw her newborn infant from the window. She is then said to have run down to the Great Hall, where she committed suicide. Her ghost is said to haunt the Tapestry Room, scene of the tragic event.

Unfortunately records do not uphold this story. Lady Mary Beauclerk is known to have outlived her husband Sidney by some 22 years and their only child, Topham Beauclerk, inherited the property from her.

In spite of this, the fact remains that there is a definite spirit presence in Speke Hall. A lady in white has been seen on many occasions in the Tapestry Room. She is said to disappear into the wall close to the window. Strange sensations have been felt not only in the Tapestry Room but also in other areas of the hall. A ghostly presence has been seen in the Banqueting Room and glimpses of spectral priests have been witnessed flitting around, no doubt from the time when Speke Hall hid priests in the many priest holes, hidden staircases and tunnels which exist behind the panelled walls. Strange whisperings, footsteps, bumps and bangs have certainly been reported coming from empty rooms.

Although history may show that the story of Lady Mary Beauclerk is untrue, Speke Hall is still a truly haunted house.

Cardiff Castle

In the first century the site upon which Cardiff Castle now stands was a Roman fort and trading post. In Norman times an artificial hill was constructed and the first part of Cardiff Castle was built. Additions to the castle continued up to the nineteenth century when the third Marquess of Bute transformed the castle into the imposing Gothic revival edifice we see today.

The number of ghostly beings who walk the corridors of the castle and visit the many sumptuous rooms can only be guessed, but the most notable of the castle ghosts is alleged to be the spirit of the second Marquess of Bute, who died suddenly in his dressing room following a banquet. This small room has since been converted into a chapel containing a bust of the unfortunate marquess on the precise spot where he died.

Another apparition of indeterminate shape or sex is said to walk the passageways of the castle. I feel that this spectre probably dates back to Roman times, before the existing castle was built.

A third ghostly visitor is a lady dressed in grey who has been seen walking past the castle and down to the bridge crossing the river Taff. She is said to pause and wave to an unseen person across the river. On other occasions she will turn and wave up to one of the castle's towers. She is usually seen at dusk.

Perhaps the best-known of the castle ghosts is the phantom coach and four. The jingling of harness and the clatter of horses' hooves, together with the sound of bells and a coachman's cry, are heard coming from the direction of a bridge. Moments later a coach and four is said to enter the castle gates and disappear. The appearance of this ghostly carriage is said to herald the death of a family member, though in recent years it has been witnessed many times and no such tragedy has occurred.

Castle Coch

Equal in beauty to Cardiff Castle and not far from it is Castle Coch. It was built in 1870 upon the foundations of a fortress some 600 years older and legend has it that a hoard of treasure was hidden in the secret passageways beneath the original fortress. However, the treasure was not discovered during the building of the castle.

A further hoard of treasure is alleged to lie hidden in the precincts of the castle. A Royalist soldier was killed at the castle during the English Civil War after hiding valuable items. His ghost is said to wander the ground floor of the castle and the grounds outside, desperately searching for his lost treasures.

A white lady is said to wander the corridors of the castle in a grief-stricken search for the son who drowned in a deep pool of water in the years before the present castle was built.

Avebury Stones

Far more accessible to the paranormal investigator than Stonehenge, Avebury stones lie on the downs near Marlborough. Older even than Stonehenge, they exude their magic and wisdom, even though of the original 100 monoliths, only 27 remain. It is indeed unfortunate that many of the ancient monoliths were smashed in the seventeenth and eighteenth centuries and used to build the farms and cottages of Avebury village.

It is possible that Avebury was first erected as a sun temple, though the facts are lost in the mists of time. Many mediums and sensitives have come up with differing theories. What is certain, however, is that the ancient stones are home to much paranormal activity; ghostly sightings having been reported consistently over the years. These have mainly been restricted to unknown monk-like spectres and wraiths. Cavaliers have been reported in the area of the stones, as they stopped off at the village during the English Civil War. One unexpected ghost of Avebury stones is that of a barber surgeon who was allegedly killed when one of the great monoliths toppled over, crushing him to death.

The Red Lion

In the village of Avebury itself is the Red Lion public house, which is well worth a visit if you are interested in a spot of serious ghost hunting.

The Red Lion's most famous ghost is Florrie, a young woman who is said to have been murdered by her husband. It is alleged that whilst he was away fighting in a war she had a love affair. Her husband discovered that she had been unfaithful and in a fit of rage put an end to her life by pushing her down a well at the rear of the old inn, where she succumbed to her injuries. The well is now located in what I assume is an extension to the original building and which now houses a dining area. The glass-covered circle of stones covered by a sheet of plate glass is the most popular table in the room!

The Red Lion is home to a number of ghosts. There is a small boy who races across the lounge area at such speed that you can feel the draught as he passes. A monk is often seen in the bar and a cavalier makes his presence known from time to time. In one of the upper rooms a spirit lady has been seen sitting in the corner, accompanied by two young children.

The only allegedly paranormal event in the Red Lion *not* the result of ghostly activity is the swinging chandelier. Unfortunately, as any diligent ghost hunter will discover, this can be directly attributed to the loose-fitting panes of glass in the window.

Plas Mawr

The house of Plas Mawr stands in the medieval town of Conwy. Robert Wynn, an influential Welsh merchant, had it built between 1576 and 1585. It is one of the finest Elizabethan town houses in Britain. It is also home to one of the saddest spirits I have heard of.

Legend tells that at one time, whilst the owner of the house was away, his pregnant wife climbed to a room at the top of the house together with their firstborn son. After some time she proceeded carefully with her descent but lost her footing on the dimly lit staircase and fell, dragging the boy with her. Both mother and child were mortally injured and were carried to the Lantern Room by the distraught servants to await the arrival of a doctor. The usual physician was not available and a young inexperienced locum named Dr Dic was sent to attend to the unfortunate pair. After an examination he announced that there was nothing he could do to save them.

On hearing this news the elderly housekeeper, in a fit of panic, fled from the room, locking the door behind her and trapping Dr Dic inside with the dead woman and child.

Later that night the master of the house returned home. He was told of the accident and rushed to the Lantern Room, where he found the bodies of his wife and his child, but Dr Dic had completely disappeared. The doors and windows were still locked; the only route of escape being the chimney. Whether he did escape or whether he died in the attempt is unknown, but the ghost of the grieving master is said to be heard in the Lantern Room, still searching for the missing doctor.

Is this story true or is it just the stuff of legend? I am sure that any intrepid ghost hunter willing to spend the night at Plas Mawr would be rewarded with more than a little paranormal activity.

Llanymynech

Home to many ghost stories, the village of Llanymynech lies in Montgomeryshire on the border between Wales and England.

The most famous ghost story of the village concerns a limestone tunnel dating back to Roman times. Known locally as the Ogof, the tunnel is believed to run for many miles under the Welsh and Shropshire hills, all the way to Chirk Castle. Horrible stories regarding the Ogof abound.

One day a local fiddler named Hugh made a wager that he could enter the Ogof and play his fiddle through the tunnel all the way down the hill and back again. Before he left, he armed himself with lots of candles and some food. He was never seen alive again.

Some time later on a dark Hallowe'en night a shepherd was passing the entrance of the Ogof on his way home and heard the sound of a fiddle playing. He looked towards the entrance of the Ogof and there stood Hugh, illuminated by a strange light, dancing and scraping away at his fiddle. The shepherd quaked with fear as he saw that Hugh's eyes were blank and staring, his face was deathly pale and his head was lolling on his shoulders as though his neck was broken. Suddenly he vanished, appearing to be dragged back inside the Ogof by some unseen force. The shepherd, thoroughly frightened, ran home.

Some years later the same shepherd was sitting in church one Sunday morning. Suddenly the sound of the frantic playing of a violin could be heard coming from the ground beneath the aisle of the church. The sound gradually progressed towards the end of the church before fading into the distance. It was Hugh, maniacally playing his fiddle whilst wandering the tunnel for eternity.

The same tunnel features in another story, that of a fox being chased by hounds. As it entered the mouth of the Ogof, it suddenly turned and threw itself into the centre of the pack. Rather than leap on it and tear it to pieces, the hounds fell back whimpering. The fox's close proximity to the tunnel had tainted it with something unknown and horrible. Its fur shone with a strange and eerie light and it gave off the stench of evil. The hounds left it alone and it escaped unscathed. But it is clear that it would have preferred to have met its end at the teeth of the pack than enter the horrors of the Ogof.

In the vicinity of Llanymynech, on a road beyond the river Vyrnwy, a ghostly horse race takes place. At one time the road was flanked by woods. In the eighteenth century a lady was returning home along the road from Oswestry market. As she neared the wooded part of the road, her horse, sensing the proximity of its stable, set off at a lively trot. As the lady tried to control her mount and manage her purchases from the market, she heard the sound of galloping hooves. Glancing behind her, she saw a phantom white horse, its head and neck outstretched as it strained every tendon in its attempt to catch up with her. Though it was saddled and wearing a bridle, there was no rider on its back.

The lady's horse, also appearing to hear the ghostly hoofbeats and obviously aware that they were being pursued by something not of this world, set off at a furious pace. It did not stop until it reached the stable yard, where it stood shaking with fear. The lady later recalled that as she neared the end of the wooded area of the road, the sound of the phantom horse ceased and it completely disappeared.

Nearby there is a house known as Siamber Wen, which is haunted by two ghostly beings, a spectral woman wearing long flowing white robes who roams the cellars and a headless figure always seen in the bedroom.

A murder is said to have taken place in this house. The story is that a nun was taken to there to attend to a woman in the throes of childbirth. The nun was blindfolded before being led down long passageways to reach the room where the woman lay. There were two masked men in the room and the nun was ordered not to speak on any account.

The nun was convinced that the newborn child would meet a terrible end, as there was so much secrecy surrounding the birth. As she completed her duties she tore off a piece from the bedding so that the house could be identified at a later date and then she returned to her lodgings.

Much later the skeleton of an infant was discovered under a slab in the kitchen. It is said that the ghost of the distraught mother wanders Siamber Wen searching endlessly for her murdered child.

Littlecote House

Curiously, a similar incident is reported to have taken place at Littlecote House, an Elizabethan manor house in Wiltshire. There, in 1575, a midwife called Mrs Barnes was called upon to tend to a lady who was in the final stages of childbirth. Just like the nun at Siamber Wen, she was blindfolded before being led into the birthing chamber. Mrs Barnes, however, recognized the voice of the man in attendance as being that of Wild Will Darrell, who was well known in the vicinity due to his harsh treatment of his tenants.

The moment the child was born Wild Will grabbed it and threw it into the fire. Mrs Barnes tore a strip of curtaining from the bed as proof of where the terrible incident had taken place.

The old midwife kept her own counsel about the events that had taken place that night at Littlecote for fear of what would happen to her. However, when she was on her deathbed she told a local solicitor and directed him to the strip of curtain material that she had taken on that terrible night. Darrell was charged with murder, but managed to escape justice by buying his acquittal.

However, he did not live to enjoy his freedom for long. One day whilst out hunting with his hounds, his horse approached a stile but shied at the very last moment, throwing Darrell to the ground. He received fatal injuries to his head. It is said that his horse had seen the ghost of a burning newborn baby. The stile became known as Darrell's Stile and it is said that on the anniversary of Wild Will's death, the sound of ghostly horses can be heard galloping around the area, together with the sound of phantom hounds searching for their dead master.

Blickling Hall

The present Blickling Hall, in Norfolk, stands on the grounds of a previous manor house said to be the childhood home of Anne Bullen, later known as Anne Boleyn, who became Queen of England when she married Henry VIII and was later executed. As already mentioned, she is seen riding in a phantom coach towards Blickling every 19 May, with her blood-ied head in her lap.

There is one more anniversary ghost to which Blickling Hall plays host. It is that of a young man who as a prank on his twenty-first birthday dressed himself in a suit of armour and plodded along one of the corri-dors towards the drawing room, where his parents were awaiting him. A year later their son died, but the sound of heavy plodding footsteps and the clanking of armour is heard on his birthday.

The south-west turret bedroom at Blickling is haunted by the ghost of Sir Henry Hobart. One day in August in the year 1698 Sir Henry challenged another man to a duel. He was soon disarmed and run through with a sword. He died the following day in his bedroom at Blickling.

The miaowing of a ghostly cat can be heard in the attics of Blickling Hall and the sound of men fighting and struggling is heard in the same area. Two servants are said to have fought over the charms of a serving girl. Both men succumbed to their injuries, but their struggles can still be heard on quiet nights.

Raynham Hall

Raynham Hall in Norfolk is where perhaps the most famous photograph of a ghost was taken. This amazing photograph was taken in 1936 when the then Lady Townshend instructed that photographs be taken of the interior of the hall. As the photographer was standing at the foot of the grand staircase the shadowy figure of a woman began to appear on the stairs. With great presence of mind, the photographer raised his camera and pressed the shutter. The resulting photograph has baffled psychic investigators ever since.

The phantom is said to be that of Dorothy Walpole, wife of Charles, second Marquess of Townshend, and daughter of Sir Robert Walpole. She was the mistress of Lord Wharton, an inveterate gambler, who was forced to leave the country to escape his debts. Meanwhile, Charles Townshend had been widowed and Dorothy Walpole and Charles married in 1712. Unfortunately Dorothy omitted to tell her new husband of her previous affair. When he discovered her secret, he locked her in a bedroom at Raynham

Hall, where she died of a broken heart. Her ghost has been seen frequently. Indeed, while staying in the state bedroom at Raynham Hall, King George IV woke in the early hours to see the spectre of a woman in a brown dress standing over him.

A Captain Marryat, whilst walking along a corridor late at night was passed by the same spectre which this time was carrying a lamp. He was so afraid that he drew his pistol and fired a bullet at the ghostly form. It disappeared.

Though the 'brown lady of Raynham Hall' is possibly the most famous spirit photograph in the United Kingdom, there are many, many examples of ghost photography. Unfortunately they are usually dismissed out of hand as being fake. Of course the possibility of a fraudulent photograph always exists, but to quote legendary parapsychologist Hans Holzer, 'Magicians and other conjurers have assaulted psychic photography as patently fake, since they could fake it. This of course is a neat trick. By suggesting the possibility as the probability, these limited individuals (spiritually speaking) miss the point. It is not what *could* be that matters, but what actually *does* happen.'

Wotton House

Wotton House in Dorking, Surrey, dates back to Tudor times, though many alterations and additions have been made to the building over the years. The long history of the Evelyn family, who lived there for many years, has been captured in the fabric of their family home. When the Evelyns finally left Wotton it was used as the Fire Service Staff College until the early 1980s.

Wotton is a ghost hunter's dream come true, with hot spots and cold spots all over the house. In the days when the building was used as the Fire Service College, many of the trainee firemen would report small objects disappearing without trace, only to reappear suddenly in another location. Windows would open of their own accord and doors would slam as though pushed by some unseen hand.

These things still happen today. But it is when the building is closed and empty for the night that the most peculiar things start to happen! When the night is still, light footsteps can be heard approaching the front door. The door is quietly opened and the ghostly figure of an old man appears. He walks silently towards a table by the fireplace in the hall. He then pauses to peer at the long-gone contents of the top of the table as though looking for some expected mail – and then he disappears! The strange thing about this phantom is that he only ever appears from the knees upwards. It is obvious to me that the reason for this is that he is walking on a pre-existing floor level.

A night porter on duty at Wotton has reported sudden temperature drops, to the point where the air feels almost frozen. One night the sound of heavy footsteps could be heard on the gravel outside. When the porter opened the door to see who was approaching the building, there was nobody there. He returned to his desk. Just as he sat down, the door opened and he could detect the vague outline of a man entering the building. The hazy figure disappeared as it began to walk along one of the corridors.

Guests who have stayed overnight at Wotton have reported a cold atmosphere and a feeling of malevolence in one of the bedrooms, yet the other chambers remain comfortable and warm. Creaking floorboards can be heard in the cold room, even when nobody is occupying it and the door is firmly closed. Anybody waiting in the small hallway outside will feel a dramatic drop in temperature, footsteps will be heard as though somebody inside the room is walking towards the door and the door handle will begin to move slowly downwards. It will then begin to move faster and faster, as though someone is making a frantic effort to escape from a locked room. Suddenly the movement will stop and all will go quiet. Any brave soul opening the door will find an empty room, though the atmosphere inside will be icy.

Losely House

Losely House near Godalming in Surrey has played host to many distinguished guests over the years. Queen Elizabeth I, James I and Queen Anne have all taken advantage of the hospitality of the More–Molyneux family, who have owned Losely since the sixteenth century.

There are many stories attached to Losely. Perhaps the best known is that of the murder of a child some 400 years ago. It is said that the second wife of the owner of Losely murdered her young stepson in order that her own child would inherit the house. Upon her husband's return he was so horrified that he imprisoned her in a bedroom, where she remained for the rest of her life. Ghostly screams can be heard coming from the room where the lady is said to have done away with the innocent child and a feeling of evil pervades the atmosphere.

There are also other ghosts at Losely. The ghost of a friendly Victorian lady has been seen outside a bathroom and a sudden drop in temperature is said to herald the appearance of a spectral woman dressed in brown at the foot of the stairs. She stares intently at anybody who sees her and then gradually fades away. A man in Elizabethan costume walks the long gallery. There are areas of the house where animals refuse to go. Many people have reported strange noises and wisps of inexplicable mist around different areas of the house.

A kindly spectral soul has been seen by children visiting the Losely nursery. They told their parents that an old lady had sat with them and watched them at their play. She did not speak but merely sat with them. They felt safe and secure whilst she was around.

Derby Gaol

Look at 51 Friargate, in the centre of Derby, and you would not know that the basement houses one of the best-known haunted locations in England. Derby Gaol was a prison from 1756 to 1828. In more recent years it was turned into a night club, but happily was bought by Richard Felix some years ago and he returned it to its former 'glory', retaining the actual cells, including the notorious condemned cell where the initials of the unfortunate inmates can be seen carved in to the heavy wooden door, and establishing a museum on the premises.

On descending the steps and entering the gaol the visitor will see the recreation area where less infamous prisoners were allowed out of their cells to work in front of the huge fireplace. Turn right and you will see cell door after cell door, behind which some people spent the last days of their physical life. Mr Felix has retained the hard wooden benches that served as beds for these poor unfortunates. The whole atmosphere of the gaol hangs heavy with past fear and sadness.

It was from this place that murderers were taken to the rear of the gaol, where they were executed by hanging or, even worse, being hung, drawn and quartered on the chopping block that now sits in the passageway of the gaol. A gallows stands to the rear of the premises, but this is a modern copy and is not the original structure where some prisoners breathed their last.

Any paranormal investigator, or indeed anyone who is looking to spend the night in a haunted property, will not be disappointed by their visit to Derby Gaol. There have been many reports of ghostly sightings and inexplicable noises there as well as strange smells and feelings. The temperature within the cells is known to fluctuate when their former ghostly inhabitants return.

Glastonbury

There is something special about Glastonbury. Few people visit this Somerset town without being affected in some way. It draws people and influences them as few other places that I know.

A visit to Glastonbury Abbey is a must. As you wander amongst the ruins of the old abbey it is not difficult to lose yourself in the atmosphere of many hundreds of years ago when Glastonbury Abbey was a busy and thriving place. Spectral Benedictine monks have been seen at the abbey going about their daily business, and there have been tales of strange events taking place, but in my opinion the 'grave of King Arthur' situated within the gardens is nothing more than a myth.

Across the road from the abbey is the George & Pilgrim Hotel. Built in 1475, it is one of the oldest buildings in Glastonbury. A ghostly monk has been seen by many people wandering around the corridors of the hotel late at night, together with the spectre of a thin elegant lady. It is said that the two were lovers. The smell of cigar smoke is often reported in the hotel when nobody is smoking and inexplicable flashing lights have also been seen.

Take a walk along Glastonbury High Street and on towards the Tor and you will eventually arrive at the Chalice Well. Legend has it that Joseph of Arimathea brought the chalice used by Christ at the Last Supper to Britain and it is hidden in Chalice Well. The water of the well stains the surrounding stones red and is claimed to have magical healing properties.

Joseph is also said to have brought with him a wooden staff, which he plunged into the fertile soil of Glastonbury. It took root and flowered and is now famous as the Glastonbury Thorn.

Standing on two ley lines (the invisible lines linking prominent features such as churches, etc.), Glastonbury Tor itself is said to be a mysterious place. At the top there once stood a Norman chapel dedicated to St Michael. It was destroyed by an earthquake in 1275 and was later rebuilt when Adam of Sodbury was abbot at Glastonbury, but has unfortunately since been demolished. All that remains is the fifteenth-century tower, which is now one of Somerset's most famous landmarks.

Glastonbury is a wonderful place, full of mysticism and charm, and I know that there are many more haunted locations in and around the town. The intrepid ghost hunter will not be disappointed.

Brodick Castle

Brodick Castle on the Isle of Arran is the ancient seat of the Dukes of Hamilton and until 1957 was the home of the Duke and Duchess of Montrose. Built around 1266 for the Stewarts of Monteith, it has a rich defensive history. During the Wars of Independence it was taken by the English and then reclaimed by the Scots in 1307. In the fifteenth century it was badly damaged by both English ships and MacDonald, Lord of the Isles. It came into the possession of the Hamiltons, who rebuilt it in 1510, only for it to be further damaged during clan battles between the Campbells and the MacLeans. It suffered yet more damage from Henry VIII's forces in 1544. By 1550 remedial work was complete, however, though the castle was once again captured by the Campbell family and had to be recaptured once more the Hamiltons. It was occupied and extended by by the Oliver Cromwell's army in the 1650s. Building works in 1977 uncovered a hidden staircase contained within the thickness of the castle walls.

Brodick is reputed to be the home of many ghosts, the most famous being a 'grey lady' who is said to haunt the older parts of the castle. She is thought to be one of three women who died of the plague in 1700. They had been locked in the basement of the castle to ensure that nobody caught the disease from them and they subsequently died of starvation.

A man in a green jacket is said to haunt the library. Who he is, nobody knows, but he is sometimes seen sitting reading in the library, perfectly at peace with the world.

There is also the legend of the albino deer which is seen only when the death of the Clan Chief of the Hamiltons is imminent.

Taking into consideration Brodick's long and colourful history, I would be very surprised if many, many more spirits did not walk within these ancient castle walls.

Nottingham Castle

This is another castle with a long and chequered history – and plenty of ghosts!

The most famous ghost story attached to Nottingham Castle concerns an area known as Mortimer's Hole, which is a tunnel carved into the sandstone upon which the castle stands. It is reputedly haunted by Sir Roger Mortimer, Earl of March. Sir Roger was the lover of Queen Isobel, wife of King Edward II. It is thought that she was responsible for the murder of her husband and that Sir Roger was her accomplice in the devilish deed. Her son, King Edward III, suspected his mother's involvement in the murder of his father and sought to bring her and her lover to justice. Using the tunnels which gave access to Nottingham Castle, he burst in on his mother and Sir Roger and arrested him. He was taken to London, where he was executed as a traitor. The ghost of Queen Isobel has been heard crying mournfully as she walks the deepest regions of Nottingham Castle.

During the reign of King John, that monarch ordered that the sons of 28 noble Welsh families be held at Nottingham Castle. It appeared that they would come to no harm. However, one day the cruel order came from King John that the boys, some as young as 12, were to be executed. They were hanged in a row over the side of the castle and their ghostly cries and pleas for mercy can be heard to this day.

The Trip to Jerusalem

Reputed to be the oldest inn in England, Ye Olde Trip to Jerusalem lies at the foot of Castle Rock, on which Nottingham Castle is built. The old inn was built in 1189 and it is said that King Richard the Lionheart and his troops drank there before going to fight in the crusades. There is some evidence that the Trip was formerly called the Pilgrim, which would tie in with other people making their way to the Holy Land.

There are numerous reports of paranormal events taking place within the building, which is built into the rock face. The most sinister apparition is that of an entity known as 'the Dark Angel'. It is said that this translucent energy takes on human-like form and hovers over an area which is believed to have been used for the practice of black magic.

On the staircase of the inn 'the crinoline lady' can be seen and in the cellar there are two further spirits. There is a small boy known as James, who is also regularly seen on the staircase. It is alleged that his parents were very strict and made him sit on the stairs as punishment when he had misbehaved. His father, Michael, is said to visit the Rock Lounge and his mother Elizabeth has been seen in the Museum Room.

Perhaps the strangest legend for which the Trip to Jerusalem is famous concerns the model of an old ship in the Rock Lounge that is supposed to be cursed. It is alleged that anyone touching it will suffer either serious injury or death. It is said that the model hung above the bar for many years gathering dust. Then the inn was visited by a health and safety officer, who noticed the dirt falling from the model and ordered it to be cleaned or removed from the premises. A medium had to be brought in to attempt to remove the curse before staff would attempt to move it. After being cleaned, it was placed in a glass case and remains above the bar to this very day. The medium, however, was not quite so fortunate. Within days of performing the ritual he was involved in a terrible car crash!

Ye Olde Salutation Inn

There are plenty of relatively recent reports of moving objects in this old Nottingham hostelry. A levitating ashtray was witnessed by a number of people in the bar at the same time. If you decide to stand with your drink at the bar, do not be at all surprised if your drink moves, apparently on its own. The bar staff are well used to glasses breaking and they are not particularly clumsy people – the glasses seem to take on a life of their own! They levitate some distance away from the shelf upon which they have been placed and then drop to the floor. This was actually witnessed by one of the regular customers.

The cellar of the inn has its own ghostly visitor. Hewn out of the rock face, it is actually a sandstone cave. Stocks of barrels, crates and the usual paraphernalia of an inn are stored there. What is not so usual is that they are constantly being moved around by an unseen presence. The ghostly inhabitant also likes nothing more than to block the exit when somebody is down in the cellar, thus causing much consternation as they try to make good their escape.

The Old Silent Inn

This old inn, situated in the middle of what is known as 'Brontë country' in Yorkshire took its name from the 'silence' of the local villagers when, in 1745, Bonnie Prince Charlie took refuge there for several weeks during the Jacobean uprisings. The name of the pub commemorates the villagers' refusal to betray him.

There is more than enough paranormal and spirit activity in the Old Silent to satisfy any investigator, but the most notable ghost appears to be that of an old landlady who had a fondness for cats. She would regularly put food out for all the wild cats in the area and would summon them at feeding times by ringing a bell from the step of a door that has now been blocked up. The sound of the tinkling bell has been heard ever since.

There is also a ghostly woman who paces up and down the restaurant. It is said that she is waiting for a loved one who will never return. A spirit male looks out of the window. No one knows what he is waiting for, but it is thought that he may have been a lookout from those long-gone days of the Jacobite Rebellion.

Temple Newsam House

The original estate of Temple Newsam in Leeds was owned by the Knights Templar, the military/religious order which guarded the pilgrim routes to Jerusalem, before passing into private hands. The beautiful old house, often referred to as 'the Hampton Court of the north', was originally built in the sixteenth century by Lord Darcey, who was later executed. It was then owned by the Countess of Lennox, Henry VIII's niece. She was the mother of Lord Darnley, husband of Mary, Queen of Scots, and father of James I. He was murdered in 1567.

The house is thoroughly haunted. Perhaps the best-known spectre is that of 'the blue lady', who has been seen in various parts of the house, particularly the Green Damask Room. She is thought to be the spirit of Mary Ingram, who was returning home one day when she was attacked and robbed by a highwayman. Although relatively unharmed, she remained very upset about the incident and spent the rest of her life guarding her belongings in an almost obsessional manner. Her phantom, dressed in a lacy shawl and a long blue dress, wanders her old home as she hunts for her lost possessions. She has been known to occasionally brush against people as she passes them on the stairs.

The spectre of a small boy has been seen appearing from inside a cupboard and walking across the room. His appearance is often accompanied by loud agonized screams.

There are more screams in the South Wing where the sound of something or someone heavy being dragged across the floor can also be heard.

The ghost of a Knight Templar has also been seen at the property. It is said that the knights were based at Temple Newsam in large numbers when they had ownership of the estate around 1155.

A monk in brown robes also wanders the grounds.

With its history and legends, seldom visited tunnels and cellars, Temple Newsam has much to offer the paranormal investigator.

Derek Acorah is the UK's favourite psychic.
Now you can enter his incredible world ...
read on for the opening chapter of the bestselling

THE Psychic Adventures OF DEREK ACORAH

First Steps

Soon after I had met Sam, my work for spirit increased. My first experience of stepping up onto the platform in a Spiritualist church was a particularly memorable one.

Gwen and I had driven to Blackpool. It was a hot sunny day and as we headed out of the seaside town we heard on the car radio that the motorways were terribly congested, so we decided that we would delay our departure in order to miss the heavy traffic. To while away a couple of hours we thought we would take a trip further up the coast to Lancaster.

We arrived in the old town around half an hour later. By now it had started to rain, so our original idea of taking a walk around the town did not seem nearly so appealing. I drove around looking for a parking space and found one in a narrow side street. As we sat wondering what to do next to kill the time, I happened to look through the rear-view mirror and saw a small building behind me. Over the door were the words 'Lancaster Spiritualist Church'.

I got out of the car, walked over to the notice board and saw that the service would be commencing in 15 minutes. We attended the Spiritualist church in

Liverpool regularly, but I thought it might be nice to join the service in Lancaster. Gwen agreed.

We walked through the door and squeezed into a couple of seats at the rear of the hall. It was very small, with a capacity of no more than 50 people. The presiding medium for that day was a lady named Gloria Duthy. I had heard of Gloria, but had never seen her work.

The service began with the usual prayers, hymns and dedications before the medium took the platform. Two or three messages had been passed on from loved ones to members of the congregation when suddenly Gloria pointed to the back of the hall and said, 'I've a man here. He's a very brusque Scot and he wants to speak to Derek!'

Gwen dug me in the ribs with her elbow, but as I have no Scottish links in my family and as Derek is not the most uncommon name, I remained silent.

'I know I'm going to someone at the back of the hall with this man,' Gloria said. 'I want the Derek who was linked to football! This spirit man is telling me to tell Derek that "the boss" is here and he's still putting the goals in the "onion bag" over there!'

Now I knew that the message could only be for me. 'The boss' was most definitely my old boss from my footballing days at Liverpool Football Club, the legendary Bill Shankly. He was the only person I knew who referred to the goal net as 'the onion bag' and it would be far too much of a coincidence to have two Dereks in such a small congregation who both had links with football and the great man. I put my hand up.

'Thank you, Derek,' Gloria said. 'This man is telling me that you shouldn't worry about not making it to the top in football. He tells me that you'll make your mark in another way – working for spirit. He's saying that you must never give up, that you must continue on, no matter what obstacles are put in your way, because you are meant to do this work. He's telling me that you should be up on this platform conducting the service. He tells me that I'm good but that you will be better. He's laughing and saying, "Just tell him it's Shanks!"'

Gloria continued with messages from my grand-mother Helen, my Uncle George and a family friend called Micky. She told me that one day my name would be in lights and that I would work for spirit in all parts of the world, and finished by asking me if she could talk to me after the service.

When the final prayers and hymns had been completed and the absent healing requests read out, I waited at the back of the hall to speak to Gloria. She was a lovely lady and congratulated me on the work that I was to do for spirit.

After a few minutes the booking secretary for the church approached us. 'I'd like to book you to conduct next week's service here,' she said.

'*Me?*'

I was overwhelmed. Although I had spent many years as a member of a Spiritualist congregation, I had never taken the platform before. Gwen was busily digging me in the ribs, urging me to agree. She had always said that I should have more confidence in myself. I reluctantly agreed that I would travel to Lancaster the following Sunday to take the role of presiding medium for their evening service.

For the whole of the following week I was extremely nervous and wasn't looking forward to our trip to Lancaster at all. Finally the day arrived. We set out to travel along the M6 but as we were nearing the service station at Charnock Richard, the car began to overheat. We pulled onto the forecourt and checked the radiator. Although there was no sign of a leak, there was very little water in it.

'I think we'd better telephone the church and tell them that I won't be able to make it,' I said to Gwen.

'No way,' she replied. 'You've said that you'll take the service and you'll do just that, even if I have to push you there in the car!'

We filled a couple of bottles with water and set off once more. We had to stop twice to let the engine cool and to top up the radiator, but eventually we arrived in Lancaster and parked up in front of the church.

As I walked in through the door my stomach was rolling and I was feeling terribly nervous. The walk to the podium seemed endless as I tottered along on quaking legs. Then the prayers were said and the hymns were sung and before I knew it, it was time for my demonstration of mediumship.

'Please don't let me down,' I begged Sam.

'Don't worry, Derek, this is your destiny,' Sam replied.

And I need not have worried. After a faltering start, the messages began to flow. I saw spirit people and I heard spirit people, and they all passed on messages of love to their family members sitting in the congregation. I found I was really enjoying myself.

Before I knew it I was being called to time by the president of the church. I received a round of applause and my heart swelled with gratitude. As I stood there on that tiny platform in one of the smallest churches I have ever been in, I knew that I had been foolish to question spirit. Those on the other side knew that I was ready to undertake platform work – they had told me so through Gloria – but I, through human frailty, had doubted it. Thank goodness that Gwen had an unswerving faith in my mediumistic abilities and had urged me to do just what Shanks had told me – to carry on no matter what obstacles were put in my way!

'People Friendly' Spiritualism

Over the following years I travelled the country appearing in Spiritualist churches in different towns. Although I very much enjoyed this aspect of my work for spirit, it frustrated me that so few people were attending the churches. At the very best, we could only expect an audience of 50 or 60 people. In those days people had some very strange conceptions regarding Spiritualism. They imagined the churches to be places where only a few rather strange people gathered to hold séances in a darkened room with a red light glowing. The hard and fast belief was that 'normal' people just did not go there, only people who wanted to 'talk to the dead'. I realized that it was time that Spiritualism took a step forward into the present day and become more 'people friendly'.

I knew that the great Doris Stokes and one or two of the better-known mediums in the UK had appeared in theatres. 'What would happen,' I thought, 'if I did something similar, though obviously not on such a grand scale?'

With this idea in mind I contacted one or two cabaret clubs in the Liverpool area to see whether they would be interested in hiring out their premises to me for an evening of clairvoyance. Unsurprisingly, I received a number of point-blank refusals, but eventually I received a positive response from the manager of the Orrell Park Ballroom. A date was arranged and a month or so later I was waiting backstage to be announced to an audience of 250 or more people.

'This is the way it's meant to be,' I thought to myself. 'If I'm to be working for spirit, surely it's part of my job to ensure that I spread that knowledge to as many people as possible.' I knew that I had been inspired to make the correct decision.

It was the first time that I had demonstrated to an audience of more than 40 or 50 people. Word had got around from people who had been for private sittings with me and Gwen had kindly offered to print off some leaflets advertising the event and had trudged around the streets of the local area putting them through the letterboxes. This was a task she undertook on a regular basis for subsequent evenings of clairvoyance at venues throughout Liverpool, though her endeavours came to an abrupt end one day when a rather sneaky dog failed to announce his presence by barking, but silently waited under the letterbox and bit the ends of her fingers as she pushed the leaflet through!

That first evening at the Orrell Park Ballroom I began my demonstration with a short talk and then proceeded to approach people in the audience and give them messages from their loved ones in the world of spirit. Time after time I was met with tears of joy and gratitude from the people to whom I spoke. It was a wonderful feeling. At the end I received thunderous applause and I knew that the evening had been a great success. 'This is the way it's meant to be,' I thought to myself ...

Following the success at the Orrell Park Ballroom I decided to move further afield. Over the next year or two I appeared at civic halls and small theatres. Audiences were growing and interestingly I noticed that they were no longer comprised exclusively of women. I also began to notice that other mediums were following in my footsteps. The word of spirit was definitely being spoken to a wider audience now!

Ghost Hunting
with DEREK
ACORAH

The UK's number one TV psychic and the author of bestselling *The Psychic Adventures of Derek Acorah* is back with more fascinating stories of his own ghostly encounters.

Also available in audio.

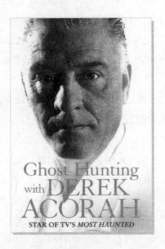

CD: ISBN 0 00 721467 7
Cassette: ISBN 0 00 720720 4